THE MORAL PRISM

THE MORAL PRISM

Dorothy Emmet

St. Martin's Press   New York

0-312-17201-X

Library of Congress Cataloging in Publication Data

Emmet, Dorothy Mary, 1904–
  The moral prism.

  Includes bibliographical references and index.
  1. Ethics. 2. Social ethics. I. Title.
BJ1012.E43   170   78-31396
ISBN 0-312-17201-X

TO ANTHONY AND ANNE

Contents

Preface

Prefaces are often partly autobiographical, telling the reader how a book came to be written. Since I have tried to do this at the beginning of my first chapter, I can concentrate here on the pleasanter task of saying thank you to various people. W. B. Gallie read most of two drafts, and encouraged me to go on. R. B. Braithwaite read two drafts, and in the course of telling me that his criticism would be likely to be the most unsympathetic I would meet, gave me a great deal of good advice. I was able to discuss Nietzsche with Peter Stern, who read Chapters 4 and 9. Thomas Baldwin read a draft of Chapter 9 and made some critical and helpful comments on some of my views on Existentialism. In themes connected with relating morality to religion, I owe more than I can specify to discussions with people concerned with the journal *Theoria to Theory*, especially Margaret Masterman. She has taught me most of what I know about the mystical thrust; that I cannot write better about it is due to my own deficiency in this kind of experience. I have made acknowledgements to a number of people concerning particular passages, including permission to use copyright material, in notes where these passages occur. In addition I want to thank Vivienne Courtney-Farrance for typing the manuscript and Gladys Keable for help in proof-reading.

An earlier version of Chapter 7 and of parts of Chapter 13 were given as the two Forwood Lectures in the University of Liverpool in 1975.

The book is concerned to attack the effects of over-simple views of morality. I try to set the stage for this in Chapter 1; in Chapters 2 to 11 I look at how some of these simplifications can cause trouble in particular spheres of interest, and how this might be combated by a more complex view. In Chapters 12 and 13 some of the philosophical chickens I let loose in Chapter 1 come home to roost, whether quietly or cacophonously I leave the

reader to judge. Since the book gives no support to fussy prop-
rieties, I hope no one will take its title as proposing an exercise in
prunes and prism.*

DOROTHY EMMET

Cambridge
June 1978

*'Papa, potatoes, poultry, prunes and prism are all very good words for the lips;
especially prunes and prism' (*Little Dorrit*).

1 Morality as Contestable

Ideally moral judgement might be a white light showing clearly what action would be best in any situation. But just as light coming through a prism is refracted into a spectrum of different colours, so our moral thinking shows us a range of different features, and attention can fasten now on one and now on another. And just as it is absurd to maintain that one colour in the spectrum is the only true, or even the truest form of light, so we must not make the mistake of assuming that one feature in the moral spectrum is the only true form of morality. The metaphor of seeing light refracted through a prism is only one way of affirming that there is always a number of features which can be seen in making a moral judgement: features which need to be distinguished, even if they also affect one another in ways that have to be specified.

Morality, then, has internal complexity and I shall try to explore this. This book has grown out of attempts to come to terms with two questions which I found I was continually failing to answer, either to my own satisfaction or to anyone else's. The first was what view of it I really held, since I seemed to switch from one view to another. The second was what to say about claims that for various reasons one can go 'beyond good and evil', or (less rhetorically) that, in some justifiable sense of 'better', it is better in some contexts to be non-moral than moral. This is partly a question of whether the scope of morality is limited. The scope may be limited if there are some situations in which no moral questions need arise. This may mercifully be so. A more serious matter is whether there may be important enterprises which can only succeed if they are independent of moral considerations, in the Nietzschean phrase 'beyond good and evil'. People who make such claims have a case, and care about important things. I knew it was no use just being shocked or indulging in moral talk at their expense. Yet there should be, I thought, some sense in which morality has the final word. It was tempting to say that this must be so if 'What ought I to do?', asked in a problematic situation, is a

1

finalising question. I cannot say that I ought to do something other than what I ought to do. Of course there can be a gap between what I think I ought to do, and what omniscience might see that I ought to do, but this gap can only be closed by omniscience, which we do not have. The issue over how far moral considerations have a final word in practical decisions is not the gap between what I think to be right and what may objectively be right. It is that the 'ought' in 'What ought I to do?' can be deliberative, and not moral. I can be considering what would be the best thing to do, but it may be 'best' for reasons other than moral ones. So what is the difference between morality and other practical interests, and is it one that gives morality priority in any way other than by definition? Thus my second question about claims to supersede morality fell back on the first, the need for a view of morality. I had to see what kind of morality those who claim to go 'beyond good and evil' thought they were superseding; whether in fact there was some other kind of morality they were not superseding; and, in the end, whether there was something about morality which they had better not supersede. There might thus be a way into morality by considering serious attempts to be amoral; taking what Socrates in the *Phaedo* called a δεύτερος πλοῦς, a second line of approach[1] where the direct approach had seemed unpromising.

Socrates gives us another remark from which to start: the discussion is about no trivial matter, but about what manner of life we should live.[2] One's manner of life can include a central thrust in the things one might want to try and achieve; the principles which guide one's relationships with other people; the basic approvals and disapprovals which underlie what (generally speaking) one is prepared to do and not to do, to put up with and not to put up with. The morality of a manner of life will need to be concerned with at least these components. They may be like the colours seen through the prism – separated so that attention can be concentrated on one of them, but if one fails to see how each component colour can modify and be modified by the others, one is failing to look on the spectrum as a whole. The spectrum and the prism through which it is perceived is an image, and like all images not to be pressed too far. It will be sufficient if it serves to point to an internal complexity of considerations for moral judgement modifying each other, it yet being possible to concentrate attention on one of them. To press the image further, to try, for instance, to make the number of considerations to which moral judgement is directed correspond with the number of colours in the spectrum, would be to labour it in an absurd way.

So we have distinguishable considerations and the possibility of concentrating attention on one or another of them. This can make for a narrowing of vision in coming to practical moral decisions; it can also mean that any such decision is open to question by those whose vision is differently concentrated. The same can be said of moral *theories*, constructed by fastening on one rather than others as the central matter of moral concern, either ignoring the others, or under-emphasising the extent to which they may make questionable the priorities in the theory. We can then get a different emphasis and a swing to another theory of a different type.

My inability to reach a moral view which satisfied me was due partly to incompetence, but partly to the feeling that these alternative theories were too narrowly selective in how they saw the moral concern. I tended therefore to be eclectic, without seeing how to defend this eclecticism.

Among the moral philosophers to whom I was exposed as an undergraduate, the most prominent were H. A. Prichard and W. D. Ross. To them the notions of duty and obligation were central, and their moral psychology was based on the belief that, unless one was completely misguided, one could not fail to recognise the general fact of obligation. Moreover, that one was under an obligation to perform acts of certain kinds, such as paying one's debts and helping one's parents, was intuitively self-evident, and the only problem in cases where two such obligations conflicted, each being a *prima facie* duty, was to see which was the more stringent. This indeed called for a judgement that was fallible, but the claims were clear to intuition.

Intuition, because no reason for the dutifulness of such acts could be given which could seem more compelling than the actual perception that they were dutiful. Hence, in the well-known article 'Does Moral Philosophy rest on a Mistake?' (*Mind*, n.s. XXI, 1912) Prichard said *yes*, in so far as it tried to derive obligations from some further notion of 'good' or some purpose to which they were conducive. Such notions of good and of purpose were not only highly elusive, but would also, Prichard held, be likely to make morality serve something ulterior to itself. Morality consisted in fulfilling one's obligations: period. And obligations were apparent, at any rate to right-minded people who looked at them straight.

Prichard's views were our main target for moral discontent in my undergraduate days, which is one reason why I am quoting them. They were an instance of a particularly clear-cut view centred on the notions of right, duty, obligation. W. D. Ross did indeed allow a role for 'the Good' as well as for 'the Right'. But this role referred to the motives of a person who conscientiously sought to do right acts, not to reasons why they should be done.

G. E. Moore went further in using the notion of Good as giving a reason for right actions; right acts were those productive of states of affairs which possessed the greatest amount of the non-natural quality of goodness. Again, this goodness was recognised intuitively. Moreover, the kinds of acts which produced it were likely to be those attained by following the generally recognised moral principles, and when in doubt one had better stick to them.

None of these views seemed to help us to live in a world where public problems—above all unemployment and the prospect of war – impinged on private problems, and where what manner of life one should live was by no means intuitively obvious. There was also John Macmurray, a moral philosopher of considerable charismatic appeal, who was saying that the notion of obligation had a place in law, but that to bring it into morals was to put oneself under a 'slave morality'. The free man's morality was to do what he deeply and sincerely felt like doing in situations in which he was open to other people in direct personal relations. Yet this early form of 'situation ethics'[3] did not help us much in thinking what to do in a world whose pressing moral problems were not just those of direct personal relations.

We have since seen a great variety of views which put the main moral weight on the expression of approvals and disapprovals, based in the end on deep-seated emotions. Moral words expressing these may then be what the late T. D. Weldon called 'shut up' words, marking points beyond which one is not prepared to argue. There is an episode in R. L. Stevenson's 'The Dynamiter' where Somerset, the hero of the story, is out with Zero, who is just about to plant his bomb. Somerset thought himself 'a total disbeliever not only in revealed religion, but in the data, method and conclusions of the whole of ethics'. 'Right and wrong are but figments and the shadow of a word; but for all that, there are certain things that I can not do and there are certain things that I will not stand.'

Yes, indeed; there can be deep emotional reactions beyond argument. But this still leaves the question of the scope of thinking in moral concerns. Does it extend further than the attempt to get as correct an estimate as possible of the facts of the situations in which moral decisions have to be made?

This was where the teleological moralists seemed to hold out more hope. The deontological moralists such as Ross and Prichard held that fundamental moral principles were intuitively perceived. To ask their point or purpose was to ask for something much more speculative and uncertain than the compelling self-evidence of the principles themselves. Yet were they indeed self-authenticating? One still wanted to ask about point or purpose. ('Deontology' was a word coined by Bentham, from the Greek *deon*, 'what is owing'. 'Teleology' is, of course, from *telos*, an end or purpose. There is also 'Axiology', a type of moral theory based on values, as approved and disapproved, however this is judged, from *axion*, 'what is worthy').

A good deal of water has gone under the bridges of moral philosophy since those inter-war years; few would want to say that the obligatoriness of certain kinds of acts was intuitively seen as factually the case. Instead we have the Prescriptivists; certain principles are put forward as choices of how to act, or as registering resolutions to act in certain ways. The appeal is to choice, not to intuitions of what is the case; but the problem remains. On a pure Prescriptivist view, what are the reasons supporting the choice of particular principles? Here the pure Prescriptivist view can be even more arbitrary than the Intuitionist, since the latter at least maintained that certain principles could be seen by anyone to be binding. And Existentialist ethics are likewise arbitrary: a person is described as making his life through choices, where what matters seems to be not what is chosen (life being as it is, this will probably be frustrated anyway), but whether the choice is genuinely *his* choice.[4]

So we come back to the question of reasons for choices, and behind that to the broader question of the point or purpose of morality. There are those who say that even to ask this question shows that one does not understand what morality is. This seems to me to be bullying. The appeal of the teleological moralists is that they are prepared to ask it; they may then refer to some master purpose to which one gives priority, to which certain principles can be shown to be conducive.

But is a master purpose a sufficient guide to what one morally ought to do, and, in any case, does one have a single master purpose? A purpose which can be used to give specific guidance needs itself to be specific. One can have such specific aims—to make money, to write a book, to become Prime Minister. One can then think out steps to achieving them; one may be mistaken about these, and of course one may fail, but calculating means can, as Aristotle (the prince of teleological moralists) said, be a matter of deliberation. And finally, one can know whether or not one has succeeded. I shall call this way of looking at purposive activity, where the end is specific and the means instrumental, Teleology A. Looking through the prism, one then concentrates one's moral sights on the worthiness of the end. But then come qualms; can any such purpose, however worthy, be given priority in all circumstances, so that its single-minded pursuit is a moral way of life? And what about the saying that the end justifies the means? Perhaps sometimes it does; but sometimes perhaps not. At least there is a question here which cannot be answered only by looking at the purpose. Moreover, what about situations in which attending to the needs of other people can get in the way of achieving it? Should one allow oneself to be deflected?

Those moralists who have looked to an end which should always be given priority have usually not specified it as in Teleology A. Their views are examples of what I shall call Teleology B, a kind of purposive activity where the manner of achieving it is a constituent part of the purpose. The plausibility of the classical kinds of teleological morality has rested on the extreme elusiveness of their ends—the notion of the *Summum Bonum* as Happiness, for instance, or the Glory of God, or Self-Realisation. Such ends function more as pointing to a general slant of mind or style of life in which one sets oneself to do whatever one does rather than as objectives to which one takes means. One lives so as to express the Glory of God, or to make people happy, or to realise oneself. One achieves such things (if one does) *in* doing other things rather than by doing other things as means to achieving them. Such purposes define the spirit in which one tries to follow one's A-type objectives, rather than being objectives on their own account.

I believe that a B-type teleology is the most hopeful approach

to the range of features in the moral spectrum. In so far as a
B-type teleology points to a purposive orientation which sets the
manner in which one goes about whatever one is trying to do,
including the making of moral judgements, it might be called a
life-style (using the contemporary vogue term) and it has been
said *'le style c'est l'homme'*. But does *any* life-style constitute a form
of morality? In a letter to *The Times* of 29 May 1976, a senior
probation officer quoted the remark of someone at a conference:
'To ask a delinquent to give up offending is to ask him to give up
his life-style.' And Falstaff expressed himself on this:

> *Prince*: I see a good amendment of life in thee; from praying to
> purse taking.
> *Falstaff*: Why, Hal, 'tis my vocation, Hal, 'tis no sin for a man
> to labour in his vocation.
>
> (*Henry IV Part I*, Act I, scene ii, 114—17)

'Vocation' is a high-sounding term. 'Life-style' is used, one suspects, by people who do not want to be thought to have anything so square as a morality. Some of the circumlocutions are
interesting. I recently had cause to remonstrate with a young
woman who was a leader of a group enjoying our hospitality, and
who were making an unconscionable noise which was disturbing
the neighbours. She said that what mattered was their relations
to each other in the group. When I suggested that relations to
neighbours might also matter, she said 'Oh yes: it would be very
anti-counter-cultural not to think that'.

There are life-styles and life-styles. Teleology B may focus our
sights on the notion of purpose in a way that may be more
adequate to morality than Teleology A, but it may still be too
narrow a focus, unless any life-style is to count as a morality by
definition. So there may be other factors besides one's way of
going about one's own purposes that may need to be taken into
account.

To count as moral, I would say that a life-style should include
considerations as to what one thinks it important to do and in
what ways; how to conduct one's relations with other people; and
being aware and prepared to be critical of one's basic approvals
and disapprovals. These ingredients are not always readily har-
monised, and some of the most deep-seated moral conflicts come
when they point in different directions.

The conflicts may be softened by teleological views which make considerations for other people into a condition for achieving one's 'Chief End'. It is said that the egoist whose aim is to promote his own interest will find that he needs to co-operate with other people if he is to get what he most wants for himself; also he will find that they will not be likely to co-operate just on his terms, so that he must be prepared to compromise. 'Jolly Miller' morality ('I care for nobody, no not I. And nobody cares for me') may not be all that jolly, unless one can be more self-sufficient than is likely. The person seeking his own salvation may be told that certain ways of behaving towards others are a condition of winning it. More subtly, a person seeking 'liberation' may be told that he cannot achieve it unless he roots out disturbing passions such as envy and anger, which are also passions that can make him behave badly towards other people. Thus a measure of social morality gets built into the pursuit of an individual end and the manner in which one goes about it. But there may be some life-styles into which not even this much of social morality is built, and we shall be looking at some of them.

Besides the ingredients which I have suggested, one might add that if a life-style is to be moral it should be serious; not the same as solemn, but carrying commitments, and this would make a place for the notion of 'ought'. That there are things one ought to do, and so limitations on one's freedom to follow immediate inclinations, is a notion to which followers of certain life-styles may well be recalcitrant. Moreover, 'ought' is notoriously ambiguous. A conversation in Trollope's novel *Is he Popenjoy?* brings out this ambiguity: Mrs Houghton says 'I'm quite sure Lord George Germain never in his life did anything that he ought not to do. That's his fault. Don't you like men who do what they ought not to do?' 'No', said Mary, 'I don't agree. Everyone ought always to do what they ought to do.' (I owe this quotation to Alasdair MacIntyre.)

'Ought' can indicate pressure to conformity, or be used as a 'shut up word'. It brings in the force of something being binding. Why should it have this force? Psycho-analysts will say that we have a strong impression of something binding because of the way in which we have been socialised, notably by our parents. We have been conditioned to feel an authoritative pressure to behave in certain ways even when we are inclined not to do so. The fully mature, if not fully analysed, person, who can say 'where super-ego was ego shall be', should be able to get rid of this feeling of pressure and of guilt in going against it. Would 'ought' then have a place in his vocabulary, apart, that is, from the deliberative 'ought'?

It might not express a feeling of pressure due to other people in the past, but a pressure one puts on oneself, in holding oneself to a commitment one has undertaken. This, however, even if it were not a commitment like Falstaff's to a vocation of thieving, could be commitment to a single-minded pursuit which left little room for consideration of other people, or for the more impersonal concerns of social morality.

A commitment to which one holds oneself can then be a factor in morality, though not a sufficient one. One may be deeply committed to some cause, and a time may come when one decides one must leave it—not without pain, and on what are believed to be moral grounds. One may undergo a conversion which leads one to change one's life-style, and this also may be seen as a moral matter. Moral commitment might be put very generally: quoting J. L. Stocks, 'he who is committed to living is committed to living as well as he can.'[5] 'Committed to living' may sound more like 'committed to jail' than following a chosen life-style. But let it mean the latter; one might live as well as one could according to one's chosen style. This might involve carrying out one's duty to one's neighbours (in the widest sense); it might be to 'serve one's generation'; it might be to go all out for some form of achievement; it might be to reach after the *visio Dei*. There are different ways in which people can envisage living as well as one can; so also different life-styles, and, again, the question of their morality. Could following the inclination of the moment count as a moral life-style, if one had deliberately decided that this is what one should do? I think if it is to count, it would have to be one's chosen way of dealing with the considerations which I have suggested come into a moral life-style; in any case, if one is deliberately trying to follow inclination, one is unlikely to be purely spontaneous.

Commitment, then, is a factor in morality, though an insufficient one. There is also the additional factor of approval and disapproval, which can be brought to bear on manners of life as well as on the worthiness of ends and the acceptability of means.

And since no way of life can be without human relationships, there is the question of what principles one may follow as one's guidelines in these.

No one can live as well as he can without some purposes (not necessarily a single one), and approvals and disapprovals will underlie the acceptability of purposes. Principles may seem more dispensable, and are indeed the factor with which those in revolt against moralism are likely to want to dispense. Principles may indeed be codifications of past taboos; they may, however, also be distillations of reflection on how, generally speaking and apart from very special reasons to the contrary, we have decided that it is best to behave. Without principles we are thrown back on first-hand appraisals under uncertainty in every situation. Sometimes indeed we have to make such decisions, and they may be crucial moral decisions, but life is not long enough, nor will decisions wait long enough, for every situation to be a matter of fresh appraisal and reappraisal, though Existentialists and believers in 'situation ethics' may think that it ought to be. Social stability surely depends on there being some ways of behaving on which generally speaking we can rely, and our own sanity surely depends on not having to agonise over every time we decide to pay a debt or to tell the truth. Principles here are more than rules of thumb. 'Rules of thumb' are generalisations about how to proceed in some form of practice, based no doubt on a certain amount of experience, but without theoretical rationale. If one can give no reasons supporting one's practical moral principles, they will either have to be rules of thumb, or taken as self-authenticating in their own right, or matters of pure choice. If they are self-authenticating, this would exclude their modification as well as their further justification. This will lead people who believe in the crucial importance of purposes which conflict with them into dilemmas which they cannot solve in these terms, and, if they believe that these are the only terms for morality, they may see their purpose as taking them outside it. What about the view that principles are not self-justifying, but are endorsed by our choices? We may take responsibility for choices after they are made, but if the making of them is not purely indeterminate (in which case one could use a random procedure for coming down one way rather than another), and if they are not guided by still further considerations of purpose or principle (which would produce a circularity), then they might be seen as preferences based on approvals and disapprovals. If these are taken as ultimate and sufficient reasons for choices, they could either be immediate intuitions of goodness and badness or be emotional reactions. Immediate intuitions might be said to be self-authenticating, but why then are there sincere differences in approvals, and why do our own approvals come to change, as they may, over the years? If approvals are based on feelings, then there is the question of whether they simply occur or whether one can criticise and educate one's feelings, and if so, how?

Moral theories based on one only of these factors of purpose, principle, and feeling, will be in danger of becoming unscrupulous, rigorist, or sentimental. These are designedly pejorative terms for the practical attitudes which can come from truncated moral views, where there is a separation of purpose from principle and principle from purpose and feeling from both. The separation of purpose and principle can produce swings between moralism and cynicism. The separation of both from feeling can not only produce hardness, but cut moral judgement off from a source of imaginative insight. The appeal to feeling alone can be sentimental if there is no way of criticising and training one's feelings. A view of morality should, I think, recognise all these features, and there is, I believe, no overall solution to the conflicts which they can produce on both the theoretical and the practical level. On both levels people will make different emphases which will give rise to disagreement and argument, but disagreements stemming from different emphases should be less stultifying than disagreements between people who see morality in terms of a single factor alone.

Thus we have purpose, principle, approval; and teleological, deontological and axiological theories of morality give prominence to one of these over the others. Some, the Aristotelian for instance, make purpose dominant and the others recessive. Other theories—we have noted Prichard's deontology—make obligations of principle the only legitimate moral concern. And emotive views, or views of the 'moral sentiments', will appeal to feelings of approval and disapproval. Yet if morality needs to comprise all these factors, an adequate theory will have to bring them in on the ground floor, not relegating one or others of them to the basement, to be brought out, if at all, only in emergencies.

So my dissatisfaction with any exclusively teleological, deontological or axiological view fed eclecticism. Eclecticism is only defensible if one can show reasons for taking different stances in different contexts—defending one's right sometimes to be deontological, sometimes not. This would mean one must be able to hold a pluralistic meta-ethics, not one in which 'the logic of ethics' is said to depend on one single principle, or in which there is a unique way in which ethical terms, such as 'right', 'good', 'interests', 'obligations', are ordered.

Here W. B. Gallie's notion of 'essentially contested concepts'[6] can be of help. (I prefer to say 'contestable' since such concepts in any actual use are not always in fact contested, though they may be.) Gallie puts as the properties of an essentially contested concept:

1. That it is *appraisive* in the sense that it signifies or accredits some kind of valued achievement.
2. This achievement must be of an internally complex character, for all that worth is attributed to it as a whole.
3. Any explanation of its worth must include reference to the respective contributions of its various parts or features, but, as these can be variously estimated, one description can set them in one order of importance and another in another.
4. The accredited achievement admits of modification in the light of changing circumstances, and such modification cannot be prescribed in advance.
5. When parties differ, each can recognize that his own use of the concept is contested by others, and has some appreciation of the different criteria in the light of which they are applying the concept. His own use has to be maintained against them—he uses it both aggressively and defensively.

Gallie cites 'Democracy' and 'Social Justice' as examples of such concepts. In Chapter IX of his book *Philosophy and the Historical Understanding* he uses the notion to attack any view of morality as defined by or dependent on a single principle. He takes the analogy of a game which can be played in different styles, the supporters of each looking to an examplar of their style to show what it means to be champions in the game. In competing to be judged champions they have to meet aggressively and defensively each other's claims as to the superiority of their respective styles.

On this analogy there could be styles in morality in which

different factors were differently weighted. Any given moral view will have its own emphasis—the emphasis, for instance, given to the more personal or to the more impersonal and public aspects of a situation; on concentration on an individual project or on the claims of social morality; on the importance of achieving certain consequences, or on deep-seated revulsions against the means by which they may have to be secured. Any view will have its own emphasis; and it will be contestable by others whose views are differently slanted.

Gallie also says that an essentially contested concept should be derived from an exemplar acknowledged by all its contestant users. I do not think that this can be said of morality, though it may be that people taking different moral stances will often acknowledge each other's exemplars as authentically moral (but I do not think we can be sure of this). Even within a particular tradition there can be different types of moral life stemming from an acknowledged exemplar. Within Christian ethics, the *Imitatio Christi* has been seen not as copying, but as something to be worked out in very different ways; though all would need to be expressions of active love, this can be expressed in a number of different life-styles.

I see the value of taking morality as an essentially contestable concept not only in giving a reason why there are likely to be different moral theories, not one of them winning general agreement, but also in its use in reminding one that there will need to be recessive as well as dominant factors in any given theory. To see morality as an essentially contestable concept is also to admit pluralism into meta-ethics, both as acknowledging different views with their own meta-ethics, and also as admitting a plurality of factors into one's own view, which will be differently weighted in the judgements one makes in different circumstances. This is not to deny the distinction between substantive morality and meta-ethics—between what in practice one thinks one should do, and what one thinks morality is like. Indeed to say that morality should be seen as an essentially contestable concept is to make a meta-ethical remark. But to see it like this will be to see it as problematic at every level; not only at the substantive level, where it is often difficult enough in all conscience (literally 'conscience') to know what one should do. Morality will also be problematic at the meta-ethical level; there will be a diversity of different stances, with different emphases, and within any recommended stance there will be no one principle which can be a sufficient guide as to what it means to act morally. I shall be looking later at attempts to set up such single guides, and the effects of following them. I shall also be trying to distinguish the kind of moral pluralism I am recommending from moral scepticism. It may indeed turn out that it is only because morality is problematic that it can have final authority.

One starts, therefore, with moral conflict as central; not just conflict between duty and inclination, which can be practically pressing but otherwise not very interesting. More interesting is conflict between different factors within morality, and conflicts between moral theories with different priorities.

I cannot therefore believe in a neutral meta-ethics. There is, of course, a distinction between general remarks about the nature of morality and actual substantive recommendations or decisions as to what one should do. The spate of books on the nature of morality shows that such general remarks can be and are disputed, so there are certainly disputes within meta-ethics. The question is not only whether meta-ethical views can be disputed, but whether differences at this level have normative implications for actual behaviour. When meta-ethicists deny this, they refer to particular prescriptions of positive morality, for instance that it is wrong to lie, claiming that this might (or might not) be said whether one was an Intuitionist, a Utilitarian, a believer in the Categorical Imperative, or an Emotivist, though one might differ in one's account of what was meant by 'wrong'. Even this agreement in positive morality is doubtful: a Utilitarian might be more disposed than an Intuitionist or a Kantian to allow exceptions to rules which he sees as on the whole leading to desirable consequences, and so might differ not only in moral theory but in overt behaviour. But the main objection, as I see it, to a normatively neutral meta-ethics is that normative ethics is not only a matter of the overt acts one thinks one should or should not do. It is also a question of the way one thinks one should go about making moral decisions. If one thinks one should try to maximise certain kinds of consequences, one's attention will be differently directed from that of the person who is concerned with cultivating pure good will. Thus a moral theory will encourage one form of moral disposition, and the kinds of action which stem from it, rather than another,[7] and this is likely to show itself indirectly, if not immediately, in substantive morality.[8] Different theories have differences of emphasis, and so each will encourage a difference in the ways in which attention is directed. This will lead to mental habits, and so there is likely to be a difference in moral psychology as well as in manner of life. The person who concentrates on duty for duty's sake will build up a different manner of life from the rational hedonist, and he again from the person concerned to maximise desirable consequences for others as well as himself, or from the person seeking self-realisation. As your manner of life, so your behaviour (even if the former is not defined exclusively by the latter).

Meta-ethical views do then have normative implications, in the conduct of life. Instead of a clear distinction of non-normative meta-ethics and substantive morality, I therefore come back to the older and more traditional notion of a moral theory which recommends a way of going about moral decisions. 'Meta-ethics' could be an analysis of the use of terms in different moral theories. Some of the remarks in meta-ethics may seem to go across the board: we may be told that in the language of morals 'good' is the most general word of commendation, and this would seem unexceptionable and applicable in different theories. But as soon as we start asking whether to say 'x is good' only means that we commend it, or whether we commend it because for some reason we think it *is* good, we are into controversial questions of moral epistemology, questions not of describing the language of morals, but of arguing a view. There may indeed be purely descriptive analyses of the ways moral terms are used in some social group, but this I see as a piece of philosophical anthropology. Such descriptions may unearth a buried moral theory in the way people belonging to such a group talk. For instance, Professor John Ladd claimed that the Navaho, whose moral beliefs he described in *The Structure of a Moral Code*,[9] were prudential materialists of a Hobbesian kind. I suspect that this is not just pure description; that most people are less sophisticatedly systematic than this in holding a moral theory, or perhaps they are more sophisticated in so representing themselves to the visiting philosopher, while not letting on about their actual diversity of moral beliefs.

So instead of substantive differences over what is right and wrong going along with a general meta-ethics which is neutral over these differences, I see morality as problematic at every level, where substantive differences affect and are affected by how people use moral terms, and where different moral theories have different normative implications as to how people set about facing moral problems

To return to Socrates: the dispute concerns what manner of life one should live. Seen philosophically, a manner of life has a theoretic structure as well as being shown in practical conduct. I have said that a B-type teleology which points to a way of life, including an attitude of mind in which one makes moral judgements, is the most promising stance for a moral theory. But all B-type purposive life-styles need not be moral, unless one defines morality as any life-style, which would be uninteresting. There are life-styles and life-styles. Can there be life-styles which are genuinely amoral?

In what follows I shall try to face this through looking at various kinds of *soi-disant* amoralism, and at the views of morality which may be their counterparts. I hope to show that no view which puts a single factor as the one essential concern of morality can be rich enough to meet the case made by some of these forms of amoralism. 'Richness' here means internal complexity, a diversity of factors which may be differently emphasised, not only by different parties in a dispute, but by oneself in different kinds of situation.

Morality, as we have it in life, is a way of thinking and deciding how we should act in connection with different kinds of human activities, needs, interests, endeavours. Its emphasis can vary with these, fastening on one factor as having priority rather than another according to these different concerns. And since no concern can be insulated from the rest of life, the priority can be disputed. Though any moral view will, on the whole, be written round one factor seen as dominant, those who hold it may find there are times when others, generally recessive, may come to the fore.

There is, I believe, no *a priori* harmonious ordering of priorities between these factors; conflict between them must be allowed for on the theoretical level as well as suffered on the practical one. If there is an ideal unity, it is glimpsed speculatively, not exemplified in practice. It is suggested by invoking transcendental notions—the Idea of the Good, the Will of God, the perfect objectively right act, even the Greatest Happiness of the Greatest Number, to name some such. (By 'transcendental' I mean that a notion is not fully exemplified in experience, and where it is not possible to specify just what it would be like to exemplify it fully.) That there are different ways in which such a notion is named itself indicates that its status is speculative. In my last chapters I shall ask whether, nevertheless, a transcendental notion, however named, has a function in morality.

To return to the moral prism. The speculative ideal might indicate the white light not revealed by the prism which is the instrument of our actual moral perceptions. Through this we see the band of colours. Sometimes they enhance each other, but more often our selective vision leads us to concentrate on one, and if we see the others, we see them as subordinate. How this happens in some of our main practical interests will be the subject of the next chapters.

2 Political Morality

That politics is 'beyond good and evil', or (less rhetorically) a sphere in which moral considerations are not applicable, is a notion with a long history. That politics may in fact be pursued amorally is not in question, but a stronger claim is sometimes made: that (sermonising apart) it is of the nature of politics that it should be so, or (if we do not want to talk about 'nature') that its distinctive purposes can only be so achieved.

This may be said in order to demarcate the study of politics as a distinctive subject. Those concerned to develop a 'science of politics' (or, if not a science, a view which marks politics out from other interests) may look for one defining factor. A favourite candidate is *power*. Politics, we are told, is 'the science of power', and power is capacity to decide 'Who gets what, when, how'.[1] The 1950s were perhaps the heyday of this view, especially in American political sociology. The works of H. D. Lasswell were prominent; for instance his *Power and Society* (Yale, 1950, with A. Kaplan) was an attempt to set out a view of politics as 'the power aspect of social process'. To say 'aspect' is to acknowledge the possibility of other aspects which may need to be taken into account if a social process is to be described in the round; it is, however, a claim that the 'power aspect' can be abstracted and treated as the political interest. If it might be said that where 'politics' means 'the study of politics' or 'political science', it can simply be confined to the power aspect, this would be to demarcate a subject-matter by stipulative definition; it is unhelpful unless it helps us understand the actual process. Another book of the 1950s, *Political Power and the Governmental Process* by Karl Loewenstein (Chicago, 1957) opens by saying that 'the basic urges that dominate man's life in society . . . are threefold: love, faith, and power', and continues, 'politics is nothing else but the struggle for power.' A rejoinder might be that surely politics is too deeply concerned with how people live for love and faith—as loyalties and ideals—not to come into it. Are they only elements in the struggle for power?

That there are struggles for power in politics is surely not in doubt. What can be in doubt is whether other interests of an ideal-regarding kind are only of political importance in so far as they can be used for these struggles so that 'the study of politics' can treat them as instrumental values. For this to be the case, politicians—or more generally, those behaving politically—will have to be skilful manipulators of 'love and faith', and those whose love and faith is being manipulated will have to be too stupid to see that this is what is happening. (Burke, who was of course no cynic, speaks of 'those good souls whose credulous morality is so invaluable a treasure to crafty politicians'.[2])

If this were the whole truth, and if politics were concerned with nothing but power, then the achievement of power would have to be the political objective as well as the political means for pursuing other objectives. Such a view would indeed set politics 'beyond good and evil', unless power could be said to be the politician's 'good' and morality seen as the single-minded pursuit of one final objective, i.e. a view which is a one-track A-type teleology.

By 'power' here is meant not any kind of effective capacity, as when, for instance, someone is said to have a power of healing, but an effective capacity where one person can influence another's choices by means other than rational persuasion. A has power over B in a context C when A is able to bring pressure or sanctions to bear to influence B's choices in respect of C.

The borderline between power and violence is thus not always clear-cut ('violence' here meaning the use of physical force which can be a threat to life, limb or property). A violent *coup d'état* can be launched for a political end, and there may be resort to violence in desperation, where rational persuasion has gone unheard. But violence itself might be called a continuation of politics by other means, as Bismarck called war a continuation of diplomacy by other means. Politics involves negotiation, possibly compromise. There are political means as well as political objectives. There are violent means, but are there also violent objectives? There can be a cult of the ennobling and therapeutic effects of behaving violently, especially for people who have hitherto been oppressed and submissive.[3] But violence as a way of life sounds like political romanticism rather than *Machtpolitik*. Violence for the sake of violence sounds perverse, as does power for the sake of power. To want power is usually to want it because of something one wants to do, and it sounds pathological just to want it for its own sake. Indeed, Lasswell, whom I have quoted, accepts this, and therefore portrays the 'political type' as characterised by 'an intense and ungratified craving for deference', a craving to be explained as due to deprivations of primary satisfactions (probably in infancy), so that primary motives are displaced on public objects and rationalised in terms of public interest.[4] Thus 'it is not too far-fetched to say that everyone is born a politician and most of us outgrow it'.[5] In other words, politics is an infantile kind of activity. This is at the opposite end of the scale from the Greek view, which saw it as the noblest of man's secular activities. I have called it a perverse view, because it singles out an instrumental value and makes it into the goal of political action.[6] 'Power for the sake of lording it over fellow creatures or adding to personal pomp is rightly judged base. But power in a national crisis, when a man believes he knows what orders should be given, is a blessing'. So Sir Winston Churchill wrote about his call to be Prime Minister in May 1940[7]—surely an adult, not an infantile remark. Politics is an activity of using power and persuasion to get policies formed and adopted in managing the affairs of some association, notably the State as the most inclusive form of association. Power enters into the promotion of policies; this is not to say that a politician is only interested in the policies for the sake of the power.

Nor is it to say that he may not enjoy the exercise of power as well as wanting it for certain purposes. Plato's saying that one can only trust people to be politicians if they would rather not be politicians is a hard one, and in any case, people who do not enjoy something are not likely to do it well. Politicians who are not just Lasswell's infantile types normally enjoy exercising power, but they want to do things with it. What they think should be done may not always be sensible, and how they see the public interest may indeed be affected by their own interests. But if it were generally understood that policies were only pursued for the sake of power, it would be difficult to commend them so as to get support. Most ordinary people are not prepared to accept a view of naked *Machtpolitik*. They want to think that the policies are in aid of objectives they themselves can support, and that these objectives are at any rate not wicked.

The pure power theorist may then say that this may indeed be true of ordinary people, but that the skilful politician knows how to use 'persuasive definitions', i.e. exploiting the sentiments which moral terms arouse in people in order to get support for things to which these terms can only be attached, if at all, in a sense very different from that in which the hearers are taking them.

The cynical use of moral language for purposes which are amoral is sometimes called 'Machiavellianism', and Machiavelli is seen as the great exponent of a view of politics as independent of moral considerations. Not, I think, altogether fairly. Machiavelli's Prince had objectives for which he had to be prepared to face danger and opprobrium. He had an ideal of *virtù*, a special kind of *noblesse oblige*. Machiavelli expresses this rhetorically, and with a contempt for the morality of ordinary people which those with democratic convictions can find offensive. But he is not putting his Prince beyond good and evil. His *virtù* is the capacity to be in control of situations and not at the mercy of Fortune. It is a Stoic quality, and goes with equanimity and indeed magnanimity (though I doubt whether the Stoics would have approved of where it leads Machiavelli). Isaiah Berlin has described this well in an article on Machiavelli in the *New York Review of Books* (XVII, 7, 1971). He looks at a number of commentators who have taken Machiavelli to be saying that the State is a non-moral artifact, and politics a non-moral game of skill; and he then says that Machiavelli has indeed a political morality, a Roman and classical one of public greatness, whose supreme aim is maintaining a strong and united *patria*. There is here, Berlin says, a contrast of two systems of values; the Christian one, centred on the well-being of the individual soul, and the classical one centred on the well-being of the State, and in the latter what is right is consequent on what is thought necessary to secure this.

Machiavelli puts this in amoralist language, as he sees 'good' and 'evil' as belonging to the morality of principles, such as truth telling, and *virtù* as the quality of the political life where success is often the reward of not being 'good' (*The Prince*, Ch.XV). Also he is writing against a background of power struggles, where the Prince's concern to maintain the strength of the State is bound up with his concern to maintain his own position. The close conjunction of public ends and personal ambition is why 'power' theories of politics are both persuasive and misleading. They are persuasive because in order to pursue public ends the politician needs to be able to get and hold power. They are misleading because this is not the same as just seeking power, and the ends pursued need not just be his own ends. But the close conjunction of public ends and power needed to pursue them can lead to a situation in which getting and holding on to power can become the dominant consideration, and this is why power theories of politics can have some plausibility; concern for a public purpose and personal ambition can be conflated, and there can be a slide from the former into the latter. It is tempting to see the moral aspect of politics as the ability to resist making this slide, and also to judge the public ends as worthy ones. Tempting, but not sufficient; for though pursuing a worthy public end may well be the dominant factor in a political morality, there is the nagging question of whether some means even to a worthy end are unacceptable either on principle or through deep-seated disapproval. And these factors may intrude and produce a conflict of conscience. This is what Machiavelli wants to preclude: one cannot imagine his Prince resigning on a question of conscience. This does not mean that his qualities of the lion and the fox are not qualities in the teleology of political morality.

There are two questions here: the notion of overriding objectives, where it is said 'the end justifies the means', and the question of whether public morality, or rather, the morality of people acting in public roles, is governed by different considerations from private morality, where they are said to act in a purely personal capacity.

I shall look first at the saying that the end justifies the means and then at the idea of a distinction between public and private morality. To say 'justifies' is to make a normative claim. If the end justifies the means, it must itself be capable of justification, or stand in no need of it. If the weight is put on the end, we have here a teleological morality of the type I have called 'Teleology A' where the end is a specific objective, and it is possible to know when it is achieved, and where the means have instrumental value. An A-type teleology need not claim that morality can be the whole-hearted pursuit of any end whatsoever. (This is a question which I shall look at more closely in Chapter 10, under the notion of 'Single-mindedness'.) There is an axiological factor in the background; the end is assumed to be a worthy one, whether as the promotion of a public cause, or of interests seen as more than personal. When the end is seen as purely the personal pursuit of power, it would be implausible to say that it 'justifies' the course taken; such and such means may be effective in achieving it, but this is a factual statement, not a normative one about 'justifica tion'. I am not concerned here with personal aspects of the morality of politicians in matters such as loyalty to colleagues and refusals to take bribes. These are indeed important matters, but the distinctive dilemmas of political morality arise over what are called 'reasons of state', where politicians claim that certain means are justified for the sake of an end which they present as a matter of their public responsibility. If they are being hypocritical over this, then it is a case of 'hypocrisy is the tribute which vice pays to virtue'. If the plea is that the interests served are more than personal the question of whether the end justifies the means joins with the question of whether there is a distinction between public and private morality. The distinction may be made by seeing private morality purely deontologically in terms of principles; public morality may be being seen purely teleologically as the pursuit of a goal such as the national interest, which is given priority over considerations of personal principle. But even if private morality is seen dominantly as a matter of principles (which need not always be the case) and public morality as a matter of purpose, in both cases there may well be problematic situations in which these kinds of morality are found to be too narrow if other factors are ignored. Moreover, taking the teleological view, I have noted that the A-type, the pursuit of specific purposes with instrumental means, tends to give way as a view of morality to the B-type, where the purpose is the promotion of a certain way of life, and the manner in which this is done is not just a means to its promotion, but itself constitutes its promotion.

Purposes in politics are in general of the A-type. There are specific objectives, and one can tell whether or not they are achieved (the curbing of inflation, for instance, or the winning of an election). There can be a number of such objectives, and they are the aims of policies. The effects of the means taken may, however, have repercussions on the way of life of the community, an A-type purpose thus affecting a B-type orientation. Political objectives can in fact be like this. A particular objective is important within a wider context of a view about the kind of community in which one wants to live or which one wants to promote. This is why some means to particular objectives may be unacceptable, and not only to people who have a deontological objection to them on principle. They are not only instrumental means which can be forgotten when the end is attained. If we are prepared to use these means—torture, for instance, to get information, or certain forms of terrorism, or secret police spying—this will affect the kind of people we become, and the kind of community we are promoting. Thus the means taken to secure a specific objective of the A-type will affect a B-type way of life. Solzhenitsyn has described in his books, especially in *The Gulag Archipelago*, how coming to accept methods of intimidation and delation can permeate the life of a whole society, so that people feel themselves in their grip, a grip which can only be broken by a colossal effort of civic courage.

So, though politics is not (thank God) the whole of life, it is not just an aspect that can be isolated from other concerns, including moral concern. Politics is indeed a use of power in order to promote policies directed to ends, but the ends have to be persuasively presented; and if the persuasion is not to be cynical (and if it is, it will probably eventually be seen through), it will be necessary to show that these ends and the means to them are consonant with the kind of community people can approve of living in. This sounds like the classical Aristotelian notion that politics is concerned with 'the good life', and indeed concern for the quality of the common life can influence the manner of politics, showing itself in public spirit as well as in public protest, and politicians can share this concern as well as being sensitive to it. Yet its maintenance as such is not, as the Greeks thought, normally the direct political purpose. Direct political purposes are normally of the A-type, where politicking is a use of power to try to obtain specific limited objectives.

Thus political morality will on the whole be Utilitarian. It will be concerned with consequences rather than with principles; and its ultimate aim (like the Utilitarians' 'happiness') will tend to be broken down into more specific aims such as welfare, economic stability, national security, these being further broken down so that 'welfare' becomes provision for basic needs, such as health and housing; 'economic stability' becomes, e.g., curbing of inflation, maintenance of investment and employment; 'national security' becomes the logistics of defence. These can become matters of particular policies issuing in particular measures.

Generally speaking, this is what we want from politics, and why (also generally speaking) the Utilitarian emphasis on consequences fits it. This may also bear on the supposed distinction between public and private morality, the distinction between people acting in public roles and in roles where they are concerned with a limited number of other people in face-to-face relations. In either case, they are agents, having to decide what they think they ought to do, and having to take responsibility for their decisions. In the public case they are having to take decisions which affect the lives and fortunes of many people whom they may never see, but whose interests they are supposed to be protecting or promoting. So it may be said that while a person may make sacrifices and take risks on his own behalf, he ought not to do so on behalf of other people—or at any rate, not without their permission.

There may be calculated sacrifices and risks undertaken for public ends in estimating consequences for the public interest. The rub is when sacrifices are made and risks taken which put public ends in jeopardy for the sake of a personal principle. There can be agonising decisions where a principle concerning a kind of act that one thinks wrong conflicts with what one thinks to be a necessary means to an approved end; this is where the politician 'of principle' will not be an unqualified Utilitarian, though he may come down on the Utilitarian side in a particular case—as Sir Stafford Cripps, when Chancellor of the Exchequer, in order not to jeopardise the financial stability of the country, denied that the £ was going to be devalued when he knew it was. This brought the problem home, because everyone knew that he was a man of high principles and a common reaction was to say, whom then can we trust in politics? But was he being immoral?

I am inclined to think that the only unqualifiedly immoral saying for a politician is '*Après nous le déluge*', since this is to express lack of responsibility. To act responsibly in a public capacity is to act with concern for consequences—pejoratively called being concerned with expediency. 'Expediency' sometimes means opportunism—a desperate attempt to snatch what may secure a short-term advantage without thought for longer-term policies. But it can also mean doing what is soberly believed to be needed for some considered and morally acceptable public end, especially to avert some public disaster. '*Salus populi suprema lex*' can indeed sound like a principle, but it is a principle prescribing the duty of doing what may be judged necessary to secure public safety.

Concern for consequences here means concern for foreseeable probable consequences of particular policies and particular decisions. This is also the Utilitarian view, and it relates primarily to specific A-type objectives. If those engaged in politics are pursuing politics with limited objectives, these may be discussed,

supported or opposed by others also using political means, and
when they are achieved or abandoned it may be possible to turn
to something else. The context of these objectives will indeed be,
as I have said, of the B-type, an interest in promoting one kind of
community rather than another. But when an ideal aim of a
B-type becomes the *immediate* objective of politics, then we are
likely to get attempts to establish the rulers' own special
Utopia—the 'godly discipline' of Calvinist Geneva, the classless
society of Communist dictatorships. Lord Eustace Percy may
have put this in an extreme way when he said, in his book on John
Knox, that 'those who seek to realize ideal aims by force of law
are always unscrupulous and always cruel',[8] but the remark
points to the fact that rigorous moralism in politics can turn into
immoralism. There must surely be something wrong with a view
of political morality which has such an outcome.

A B-type orientation will of course suggest directives for A-type
projects, and indeed it is proper that it should do so. For instance
the Benthamite concern to promote the Greatest Happiness
marched in Benthamite programmes with exact and detailed
schemes for such things as model prisons and ballot boxes for
elections. But to try to produce legislation directly to promote the
Greatest Happiness of the Greatest Number would have run up
against the difficulties not only of applying a felicific calculus
except in very limited situations, but also of whether happiness
can be commanded. Enforceable political objectives have to be
limited; ideal aims are not so limited, and generally depend on the
existence of a particular motivation.

A political theorist with a strong revulsion against attempts to
implement B-type purposes by political means is Michael
Oakeshott.[9] Indeed, he would like to restrict the notion of politics
to the rules for procedural practices of a form of civil association
rather than let it be used for the pursuit of any substantive
objectives even of the limited A type. For him procedure is dominant and purpose recessive—if it cannot be entirely bred out, at any
rate the less of it the better. Political utterances should be concerned with 'the engagement of considering the conditions of
association (i.e. its rules etc.) in respect of their desirability'
(*Political Studies*, XXIII, 4, p. 411). They should not be concerned
with 'the engagement which seeks to determine who gets what,
when and how as the contingent outcome of the operation of these
conditions of association' (ibid., p. 414).

This makes for a curious analogy, in highly moral terms, to the amoral doctrine of power for power's sake. In this an instrumental means was sought for its own sake. Here we have the notion of procedures in a legal and constitutional system which prescribe the structure through which people living within a shared tradition express themselves in their relations to each other. 'Express', rather than 'want to do things together'. We have a picture of the desirability of maintaining certain kinds of procedure; that we should ask 'what do we want to use the resources of the State for?' is to try to turn a civil association into a commercial type of enterprise. (Would it indeed on Oakeshott's view have any 'resources'?) Oakeshott sees that it will be difficult for people not to want to do something through the State besides maintaining a legal framework within which they can follow their own avocations. He therefore thinks the modern State is a (regrettable?) hybrid of civil association and what he calls *universitas*, his term for an association formed for purposive enterprises.

It may well be that the notion of an overall Purpose (with a capital P) of the State may be dangerous, presenting a B-type ideal aim in terms appropriate to A-type objectives. It may also be that what A-type objectives should be pursued through the State may be a contingent matter, varying in different times, and no one of them need be by definition of the 'essence' of the State, though there may be some, such as defence and public order, which would seem to be pretty constant. Oakeshott is calling attention to the context of ways of life in a civil association to which certain constitutional procedures can be appropriate (did not Aristotle indeed say that a constitution was a way of life?). But procedures are there to enable substantive things to be done. If what it is appropriate to do varies with circumstances, this does not mean that it may not properly be done through the State.

We have, therefore, the social context of a way of life, the maintenance of which is a matter of B-type teleology, and the pursuit and enactment of specific A-type objectives. This is why I think Utilitarianism can answer fairly closely to the morality of politics. It has a B-type ideal—in the case of classical Utilitarianism the pretty vague one of 'happiness'. In politics, there can be attempts to translate some of the more obvious likely ingredients of this into more limited terms such as welfare, stability, health; and these can then be further broken down into measures which can become matters of political decision. I am taking Utilitarianism here as a view that what is right and wrong is judged in relation to consequences. I am not taking up the particular problems of strict Utilitarianism about the measurement of utilities, and especially of interpersonal comparisons of utilities. Nor am I concerned over the elusive character of happiness. I am only concerned with measures which can reasonably be assumed to make for desirable consequences and can be specified in such ways that something can be done about them by political action. It may be said that this is only a crude Utilitarianism, but it may answer to the kind of consideration of consequences which has to be taken in political decisions.

This Utilitarianism can, of course, be of a public-spirited, not an egoistic type, and it may have its limitations as a complete view of personal morality, in that a decision of conscience as to what a person is prepared to do may cut across his estimate of desirable consequences. It is a morality, but one which concentrates on the factor of purpose, and dismisses principles except in so far as they minister to a purpose. Yet it may not be possible always to repress these, or make them thus subordinate, and when they break out there will be dilemmas of conscience against some means to an otherwise acceptable end.

This is not to say with Kant that some principles—telling the truth, for instance—should always be observed. This would limit the moral concern in the opposite way. The question is whether taking certain means to an otherwise desirable end can produce such an acute problem of conscience that a person may say that if this is what he is required to do, then he is off. Jonathan Glover, in a paper entitled 'It makes no difference whether or not I do it' (*Aristotelian Society*, Supp. Vol. XLIX, 1975), calls this 'the Solzhenitsyn principle', quoting from Solzhenitsyn's Nobel Prize lecture: 'Let the lie come into the world, even dominate the world, but not by me.' Glover calls this 'moral self-indulgence'. Yet it need not be a concern to keep one's nose clean rather than to take political responsibility (and Solzhenitsyn is not saying that it is *desirable* that the lie should come into the world through other people). There may come a point where a person's whole integrity is involved in refusing to co-operate. This is put negatively. There is also the civic courage to take a stand in ways which put one's own political future at risk, and sometimes, if not at once, the protest may have a positive political effect.

This is where the stickler for principle rather than purpose can make his point, though he may not make it in the right way by asserting absolute principles. There is a temptation to cite absolute principles, since on a more complex morality it is not at all easy to say where principle ends and expediency, even ambition, begins. There is a slide from the expediency of public concern to the expediency of personal opportunism. This may be best resisted by one who knows that beyond immediate objectives, beyond the social purpose of sustaining a certain kind of community, beyond even any code of principles, are a person's own ultimate convictions as to what he is and is not prepared to do. We may call this his conscience, and this need not just be a socialised super-ego. It can be judgements coming from the root of his own integrity. There may not only be some particular actions, but also some ideals of a social purpose that a person finds so repellent that where political opposition fails he can only fall back on his moral integrity and withdraw from political co-operation, turning to active or passive resistance. Indeed in this he may serve the cause of politics, for if politics is not the whole of life, it needs to be brought into focus by people setting their sights beyond it. Plato indeed said that politicians should look to a good beyond politics. There is, I believe, a crucial difference between those who know this, however they may express it, and those who are solely preoccupied with politics, its fixings and compromises.

The person who has a conflict of principle over a political course may be reminding himself and others of this wider context. This is not saying that political problems can be solved by simple moralism, still less by moral pronouncements, a course that can lead to self-righteousness, 'the inevitable result of an over-simple moralism' (a remark of Reinhold Niebuhr in connection with John Foster Dulles). Those who are prepared to go into political conflicts, which are conflicts of power as well as of persuasion, and who yet keep their moral integrity, will not make judgements such as the leaders of Moral Rearmament made in the 1930s, when they said that Hitler could be stopped by 'absolute honesty and absolute purity'. 'Politics', wrote Reinhold Niebuhr, 'will, to the end of history, be an area where conscience and power meet, where the ethical and coercive factors of human life will interpenetrate and work out their tentative and uneasy compromises.'[10] Reinhold Niebuhr was not the cynic he has sometimes been taken to be, and which may have been suggested by the title of the book from which this quotation is taken. He spent his life struggling with the over-simple moralism of certain kinds of liberalism and pacifism. But he cared that even the 'uneasy compromises' should be seen as genuine struggles of conscience. He also had a passionate conviction of the importance, even for politics, of a vision of a deeper kind of personal morality. To quote him again, this time from a later and more mature book:[11]

> Humanity always faces a double task. The one is to reduce the anarchy of the world to some kind of immediately sufferable order and unity; and the other is to set these tentative and insecure unities and achievements under the criticism of the ultimate ideal. When they are not thus challenged, what is good in them becomes evil and each tentative harmony becomes the cause of a new anarchy. With Augustine we must realize that the peace of the world is gained by strife. That does not justify us either in rejecting such a tentative peace or in accepting it as final. The peace of the city of God can use and transmute the lesser and insecure peace of the city of the world; but that can be done only if the peace of the world is not confused with the ultimate peace of God.

This gives a picture not of politics as beyond good and evil, but of a good beyond politics which politicians can acknowledge, and thereby bring their own task into perspective. The reference to St Augustine is instructive. St Augustine's Christian and Platonic picture of the 'City of God' is not just an ideal contrasted with the depravity of the world. Justice and peace in the earthly city are rough justice and precarious peace, but they are partial expressions of the aspiration towards the City of God. It will be an illusion to think that the institutions of the earthly city can be so arranged that they will be completely harmonious so that no tensions need arise, so that what Marxists and Existentialists call 'alienation' could be avoided. For St Augustine, as 'strangers and pilgrims' we must always be prepared to carry a certain amount of alienation. The conditions of actual social life are such that we can never be completely at home in them—at least if we have the further vision suggested by 'the City of God'; and it may be that the vitality of actual social life can draw on the resources of this further vision.

I first read St Augustine's *City of God* in Healey's Elizabethan translation in September 1939 in a first aid post in the University of Manchester waiting for the air-raids which, at that stage of the 'phoney war', did not come. I do not know how far this great epic of 'that most glorious society and celestial city of God's faithful which is partly seated in the course of these declining times' depends on the doctrines of predestination and the punishment of the human race for Adam's first sin. What I took from St Augustine was the difference between the two loves which inform the earthly and the heavenly cities, and how both are involved in the life of politics.

One can see the contrast in social philosophies and also in religious ones which have shed this concept of the City of God, a good beyond politics however named. Harvey Cox, for instance, in his book *The Secular City*[12] takes the powerful image of 'the City', but this is not an image of a religious ideal; it is its own secular self. He does not see the traffic of Jacob's ladder pitched between Heaven and Charing Cross. He sees Charing Cross, and he likes what he sees. He does indeed moralise politics, but he has lost the Augustinian vision which Reinhold Niebuhr had for my generation—a vision of how members of a society may be deeply engaged in its conflicts, without seeing them as total conflicts between forces of light and darkness, because they share a common penitence and a common aspiration. Power, coercion, even intimidation may be words which indeed describe aspects of politics, but they are not the last or the only words.

If they are not this, then politics will need to be nourished from some root—I am prepared to say a mystical root—which is not itself just political. We come back to the 'faith and love' which our American political scientist repudiated as factors in politics. Charles Péguy, the French Catholic poet and political radical killed in the First World War, saw that there was a dialectic of *mystique* and *politique*. *Mystique*, as vision prepared for sacrifice, nourishes *politique*—but *politique* can exploit vision and sacrifice. 'Everything begins in *mystique* and ends in *politique*'. 'The Republican *mystique* was when one died for the Republic; in the political republic, the republican *politique* is, as at present, that one should live off it.'[13] James Cameron (I think) has translated *politique* as 'jobbery'.

A simple moralism of rules is not likely to stop this slide. Politicians may indeed take the slide because they see the inappropriateness of a purely rule-bound morality. A morality which makes its dominant concern responsibility for the consequences of one's decisions on the lives and fortunes of others, and which helps its adherents to use power without self-aggrandisement, will be more complex, but none the less a morality. It may be that the more complex a morality, the more it calls for moral courage as well as intelligence, and moral courage needs to be sustained from a root beyond the life of politics. Otherwise tough-mindedness can become cynical, and clear-sighted realism a manipulation of interests.

Politics is perforce a sphere in which the factor of purpose is dominant, and where purposes are normally A-type objectives pursued against opposition. But they can be pursued in an attitude which comes within B-type teleology: a concern for living in a certain kind of moral community. Some methods of pursuing A-type objectives may then be seen to be such as to destroy the B-type objective of maintaining the way of life of a particular kind of community, and so also to destroy a source of criticism of politics which can sustain it as a matter of argument and persuasion as well as of power. Yet even the values and traditions of a particular community may not be the final source of criticism. These may themselves be called in question by people whose judgement springs from the root of their own moral integrity. Without the civic courage which comes from these sources of criticism, the life of politics itself can be lost in a police state. By going beyond good and evil politics may, therefore, end by going beyond itself.

3 The Moral Context of Science

There is a large literature on 'Science and Ethics' and nowadays a growing one on 'the social responsibilities of science' (or better, scientists). I shall not enter this discussion in any detail; it is of interest to my purpose only if it can be seriously contended that doing science puts a person beyond moral considerations.

It may be said that whole-hearted concentration on an exacting kind of work leaves neither time nor energy for personal relations other than those which serve, or at least do not disturb the work. If this claim is made, it would be an instance of an A-type teleological morality, where absolute priority is given to single-minded pursuit of one specific purpose. It is not a moral question peculiar to the pursuit of science, and it is likely, I think, to come up in this extreme way in the lives of artists rather than of scientists, since the former can be working individualistically, while scientists are almost always working in some kind of collaboration. There is, therefore, not only the morality of the inner discipline necessary for concentration of a purpose, but the morality of relations with colleagues more and less directly involved in the same enterprise. The former can be put under a moral rubric such as 'devotion to truth', and, in general, what Aristotle called 'intellectual virtue' ($\delta\iota\alpha\nu o\eta\tau\acute\iota\kappa\eta\ \acute\alpha\rho\epsilon\tau\acute\eta$), shown, for instance, in the obligation not to fudge one's results. The latter, the inter-personal side, produces questions of behaviour towards collaborators, colleagues, rivals, and the wider scientific community, which need to be answered in one way or another. They have traditionally been answered by looking on the scientific community as one which is open and international, where results are made available in publication and personal communications, and where acknowledgements should be made and other people's results not plagiarised. There are, however, voices saying that this unwritten code cannot survive in a highly competitive scientific world, where people are looking for prestige jobs, if not Nobel Prizes, and where it is a race to get in first. This was put explicitly by James Watson in *The Double Helix*: the person who suffered in this particular instance was Rosalind Franklin, and the ethics of this controversy have been given a close look by Anne Sayre in her book *Rosalind Franklin and D.N.A.* (New York, 1975). Such behaviour stems from moral cynicism rather than from a philosophical defence on the grounds that science is 'value-free'. The concern is that one should be the first to make a discovery and get the credit for it. If it is said that science will be more vigorously pursued under the incentives produced by amoral competition, then the opposite case could be argued: 'Keep your mouth shut and your drawers locked' could hold up the flow of communication which feeds its promotion. These are contingent questions about what facilitates the growth of science; they do not show that because a scientific view is not itself moral or immoral, the *pursuit* of science is inherently amoral.

Moral questions also come up over the applications of scientific work. As I have said, a great deal is being said and written nowadays, both in the national press and in papers such as the *New Scientist*, about 'the social responsibilities of science'. I should prefer to say 'the social responsibilities of scientists'. There is no question but that social problems are produced by scientific developments—problems of radioactive waste, atmospheric pollution, dangers in genetic engineering, and so on. Scientists may say that their responsibility is to get on with their work and that problems produced by its applications or its by-products are not their concern, but those of government or industry. But these latter cannot cope with the problems without the collaboration of scientists, and if scientists need the support of a social morality which allows freedom of thought and movement, can they claim to be immune from concern with matters of social morality in the applications of their work, even though they may choose to ignore them?

They are, I think, usually aware of this. The grislier experiments, for instance on brains of monkeys, may be defended not by saying that the infliction of suffering is justified if knowledge (any kind of knowledge?) is advanced but by saying that the particular knowledge gained may have medical results of value to human life. The defence may be unsatisfactory, but it is an attempt at some sort of moral defence. And when experiments are done on human beings in concentration camps, in prisons or in Soviet psychiatric hospitals, the authorities responsible, and no doubt the scientists they employ, will claim that these people are enemies of the State who have forfeited their human rights.

Far from saying that the pursuit of science is immune from morality, scientists are more likely to say that we need a new morality for a scientific age, based on factual appeal to consequences, and not on what is thought to be a residue of religious authority. Such a moral view is likely to be a fairly simple form of Utilitarianism, appealing to factual consequences which are likely to promote happiness, happiness being something not only easily recognised, but whose desirability can be accepted as a non-contentious fact. When one gets beyond this simple notion of happiness, there are questions over 'happiness in *what*', over conflicts between one person's happiness and another's, over how one estimates and compares happiness. These are familiar problems for Utilitarians.

Some, however, who want a humanist morality for a scientific age may go about it in the opposite way. They may start from the separation of fact and value, the 'autonomy of ethics', the view that no proposition stating what ought to be done can be derived from a proposition stating what is the case. What ought to be done, therefore, registers a decision on the part of the agent. Such a view does not down-grade ethics in the name of science; it puts the weight on our responsibility for making moral decisions, and the more it is said that science is value-free, the more this responsibility is laid on us. The distinction of facts and moral choices need not, of course, mean that facts are irrelevant to what is chosen. Science can enlarge our understanding of facts such as those of our own psycho-physiological nature, and of the ranges of likely consequences of courses of action, and in such ways helps us to make wiser choices. (There are also questions of fact and value which can be matters of the metaphysic of morals, and I shall turn to these in a later context.)

I do not think, therefore, that there is a 'scientific frontier' of morality in the sense that in general scientific work can only be properly done if morality is left behind. Scientific work is likely to be less rather than more productive without the internal integrity of scientists in their own work and in their relations with one another. Beyond this, the problems raised by the applications of their work in the wider community may be contingent as regards the actual work of discovery itself (though they may affect what the community is prepared to fund, which may be a necessary condition, in a non-logical sense of 'necessary', for some kinds of discovery). The scientist who says that applications are not his concern, but those of governments or industrialists, may be taking a narrow view of his moral responsibilities. But he is unlikely to take a high line and say that they are not his concern because his work puts him beyond good and evil.

There might, however, be a high line. There might be what we may call the 'Faustian' scientist, who is prepared to go to all lengths morally for the sake of some discovery. Faust knew what he was doing. He knew he was making a pact with evil; he did not claim to be beyond it. If the Faustian scientist does claim this, then what he is doing is to make his desire for knowledge his ultimate concern, holding that he is justified in pursuing it at the expense of other concerns. This, I have said, is an extreme A-type teleology in morality, fastening on one aspect alone of that essentially contestable concept. Such a teleology produces problems as a moral view,[1] but they are not problems which arise peculiarly because the end pursued is the advancement of scientific knowledge.

There are indeed, particular problems which come up in the social sciences, where the subject-matter is human beings and their relations to each other. Since this is so, the investigator himself is in a personal relation to his subject matter in a way in which the natural scientist, bombarding atoms or being beastly to bacteria, is not. Mutual trust, respect for privacy and confidentiality, can produce obligations for the investigator which he may disregard out of insensitivity, or because he thinks his subjects will not be in a position to answer back. If he defends his behaviour by claiming that obtaining knowledge, just as knowledge, has an absolute priority, then he is asserting a purely A-type teleology as his moral view. If he says he needs to get the information for political or commercial reasons, then the dispute will be over political or commercial morality, and not over the moral immunity of scientists.

In the human sciences, there is a further question of subject-matter: moral beliefs and practices can be part of this subject-matter, so that if the way in which a social scientist envisages these is inadequate, it may affect his theoretical conclusions as well as his relationships with the people he is studying. This is presumably not a factor in the natural sciences, but it may well be one in the human sciences. In the case of Sociology, few indeed would dispute that the actual forms of social action studied have their moral aspects, or say that *Homo Sociologicus* need not be a moral being. Indeed Durkheim, the founding father of modern Sociology, presented social life as predominantly a moral discipline. More recently, however, sociologists have tended to present the morality of the people they study as a fairly narrow kind of self-interested Utilitarianism, not, I suspect, because it is generally found to be like this so much as because of an assumption that a tough-minded motivation of this sort is scientifically respectable, if not self-explanatory, in a way in which more altruistic kinds of motivation would not be. Thus the interest of a method of approach may be affecting the way a subject-matter—in this case moral behaviour and motivation—is seen, so as to make it minimally significant.

It is sometimes thought that the social sciences are committed, *qua* sciences, to a deterministic view of actions. This is not a view I find plausible;[2] in any case it is not the question I am here concerned with, which is whether the pursuit of certain kinds of activity justifies a person in saying he can be outside the scope of moral considerations recognised in other spheres. The deterministic view is not one which puts particular activities outside morality, but one which puts morality itself out of court, except as a description of forms of social behaviour induced by sanctions. What I think can be said, even if one rejects sociological determinism, is that the findings of the social sciences can show institutionalised structural constraints on the effectiveness of actions. We often have less room for manoeuvre than we would like to think, if we do not want the results of our actions to be frustrated by circumstances outside our control, or to be as unwelcome as they are unintended. This is not to take away moral decisions, but to supply greater realism about the contexts in which they are made, and this is especially relevant in the case of economic policies. If Economics is to be classified among the social sciences, it is marked out in having a much greater exactness and mathematical development, as well as producing, if not what some of the old classical economists called 'iron laws', at any rate mathematical correlations of variables from which deductions can be drawn.

It used to be assumed that *Homo Economicus* acts from self-interest: contemporary economists might rather say, in order to maximise his preferences. There is a certain circularity here, if 'preferences' are defined as choices revealed in economic behaviour. Speaking of 'revealed preferences' is a way of saying that economics as a study need not be concerned with inner motivations, as facts of mind, but only with their manifestations in economic activities. I shall return to this later. First, however, we need to note that the abstractions under which economic activities are studied are not a complete account of the conditions which make these activities possible in their actual social setting. Economic transactions go on within the institutional context of a society which includes a legal system giving protection to property, and, in the more developed societies, providing for a law of contract, if not regulations about fair trading. Durkheim pointed out in *The Division of Labour* that as societies advanced from simple traditional forms centred on extended families to the condition of a market economy, their stability would depend on contracts. Though these might sometimes need to be legally enforced, if there were not a general presumption that most contracts would be observed without recourse to law, there would not be enough confidence to sustain a trading community.

So a background of social institutions maintaining practices with moral as well as legal aspects is needed as the milieu for economic activities. Adam Smith has been looked on as the father of the view that in an economy based on the division of labour people by acting purely from self-interest could also promote general prosperity. But he was also well aware that the economic activities of individuals in a free market went on in a society where the State provided defence and public services, such as the maintenance of courts of law and the Watch, which was the precursor of the police force, and that these had to be supported through taxation levied on principles which needed to be accepted as equitable

Nevertheless, economic activities are activities of a particular kind, broadly those concerned with transactions over scarce resources, their characteristic form being that of an exchange where A provides something for B and B provides something for A. Thus, each has an interest in getting something he wants, and, though he may be concerned over the satisfaction of the wants of the other, he need not be so concerned. Each may be acting from self-interest, or if another motive is present, the economist need only see the exchange as a way in which A reveals his preference for what B can provide and vice versa. That is to say, the concern is not with what motivates preferences, but with the choices to which they lead. Weber's Puritan businessmen may have made money not because they were moved by cupidity, but because they thought they should live disciplined hard-working lives for the Glory of God. But make money they did, and economic historians study the interlocking effects produced by the ways in which they made it. So it may be said that economic studies are interested in motives not for their moral praiseworthiness or otherwise, but in so far as they lead to a form of economic activity, as, for instance, when a motive may be seen as an incentive.

This can be said; but it is not the same as saying that economic activity is by definition self-interested. It can be geared to social goals. Welfare Economics not only presupposes a social system, with its support for and restraints on economic activities, but it is also concerned with recommendations for implementing social policies, so that it is studied within the context of goals judged to be socially desirable. It might be said that its value commitments are only hypothetical—granted these goals, recommendations can be given on economic measures designed to implement them, so that the economic side of the story is concerned with instrumental means. Whether the economist can restrict his responsibilities by thus restricting his role is a question, I have noted, which also comes up in the case of the natural scientist, who operates in a social context. Welfare economics in addition recognises this context by harnessing economics to social policies. In the case of market economics, the social context might be regarded simply as the field for economic activity, and an entrepreneur may quote 'Business is Business' to the effect that such ventures can only succeed if they are not morally restricted. If he behaves unscrupulously, he might say that other people would do the same to him if he did not outwit them. If he goes on to say that they have as much right so to treat him as he them, and so he does not complain about them, he is at least subscribing to the Universalisability which is said to be one criterion of moral judgement.[3] Beyond this, it is likely that he is going in for practices which he himself thinks are immoral, and that he has grown a thick skin. In some cases he may think that what he is doing is necessary for the survival of his business, and with it the good of his family and his work-force. He may or may not be correct to think so; he may genuinely find himself caught in conflicts between incurring risk of disaster and observing a principle he generally accepts. In this case his position is analogous to those which produce the problems of political morality. But if he does not recognise that there is a problem, and does not turn a hair over what he is to do, I suggest that he is simply deciding to be immoral.

Therefore, I see no special consideration peculiar to economic activity which puts it outside morality. If it is said that it is only successful when free from moral restraints, I have questioned whether, apart from what ought to be, this is in fact true as an empirical generalisation. Fred Hirsch, in *Social Limits to Growth* (London, 1977) maintains that the economic expansion of a free market, as advocated by Adam Smith, only worked successfully because a good deal of pre-bourgeois moral restraint could still be presupposed. He goes on to say that we are now in the precarious position of living in a period where the older moral restraints are being corroded, and where unrestricted expansion can lead to frustration (the more cars, the worse the traffic jams; the more people owning second homes in the countryside, the more congested the countryside, and so on). Restraints in the name of altruism and public spirit are not negligible, but not likely to be strong enough to carry the whole weight; the characteristic economic appeal to rational prudence may be more effective. It will need to be a disciplined prudence which looks beyond immediate advantage (the problem of trying to curb inflation through persuading people to accept a policy of restraints on incomes is an example).

Rational prudence may not be the highest form of morality, but it is not to be despised. It can be extended to apply to ways of behaving which are not restricted to personal advantage. It is a Utilitarian view, and, as with politics, the form of moral theory most applicable to economic activities is Utilitarian, the more so in that they are often concerned with measurable utilities. They will not, however, be limited to this concern. The management of a firm, for instance, will be involved in relationships with their work-force, their directors, investors, the Government; and these involve actions which have a political as well as an economic character. So the achievement of the purpose of maximising some utility cannot be insulated from other factors to do with human relationship, which, as in politics, can raise questions of principle as well as of purpose.

I have given more space to Economics than the other social sciences both because, scientifically speaking, it is more developed, and because it studies a particular form of practical activity, whereas there is not a 'sociological activity' as distinct from doing Sociology. Economics as a theoretic study can analyse economic activity in a value-free way, except in so far as the study, like any science, involves values like intellectual honesty and fairness to colleagues in how the work is done. It may indeed be used for policy recommendations in connection with social goals, but the actual analysis is distinct from the policy which recommends it. It studies an activity which presupposes human motivations, but these are of interest to the analysis only as revealing preferences. With some qualifications it might therefore be said that the study itself abstracts from moral considerations. Nevertheless, the actual activities studied by the economist can only operate in a social context embodying certain moral restraints. If a person claims that because his activity is economic, he is justified in being amoral, he is claiming the right to transfer the abstraction made in the theoretic study to the practical operations. This does not constitute a philosophical case for saying that economic activities *per se* can claim moral immunity, especially since, if they are not to founder as enterprises, they depend on moral underpinning in their social context.

To summarise: economic choices reveal preferences, preferences are whatever people prefer, and there is no need to make them self-interested by definition. They may be, for instance, to promote a charitable fund, or to invest in a workers' co-operative from interest in a social experiment, and such enterprises are not always economically unsuccessful. Moreover, the empirical conditions in which economic enterprises prosper are likely to include a presumption of confidence, in such matters as that contracts be kept. This suggests at least a Hobbesian prudential morality; and it is arguable that a general presumption that 'men shall keep their covenants made' needs willingness to maintain it which does not only depend on continual surveillance. At least, I see no case for arguing that economic activity in its social context presupposes absence of moral constraints. If a person says that others can take care of these while he pursues his economic aims, he is being parasitic on this context. This he may well be, and if he keeps within the law or manages to evade it, he may have some success. But as with most parasites, success is likely to depend on there not being too many of them, or they will kill their host.

4 The Aesthetic Alternative

If we are looking for ways of life in which situations, actions, characters, are evaluated in manners alternative to the moral evaluation, the aesthetic way would have the strongest claim. Strongest, because it has its own standards of better and worse, and because it can be an orientation to the whole range of experience.

To say that there may be an aesthetic way of life is to say more than that ways of life and the actions which happen within them can be appreciated aesthetically. Appreciation is a spectator's response; the question is not whether a spectator appreciates an action aesthetically, but whether an agent judges what he should do in aesthetic and not in moral terms. 'Good' would then be a term of aesthetic approval, and its opposite would be not 'evil' but 'bad'. In a later context I shall be asking whether it is significant that 'good' in its moral use has two contraries, 'bad' and 'evil'. Here I am concerned with aesthetic evaluation, and I do not think that 'evil' would be used of a work in its aesthetic aspects. Clearly there can be aesthetic expression of evil, and it can make for great art. Such art helps us to understand the evil, but (unless we are confirmed Platonists) understanding need not necessarily imply moral approval or disapproval. Moreover few would want to say that moral considerations should govern aesthetic approvals (Tolstoi was perhaps the last notable artist to say this, though there have been critics, such as Matthew Arnold and F. R. Leavis, who have seen aesthetic criticism in highly moral terms). Aesthetic appreciation is turned towards looking, enjoying, perhaps understanding. What is appreciated may have moral content; indeed serious art, especially in novels, is likely to have this, since it probes into the complexities of human conflicts, achievements, failures, passions. If the artist can help us to see what these are like, he can give us a prolegomenon to morality. Moreover, works of art need not be morally impotent, even if aesthetic judgement of their merit as works of art differs from moral judgement on the kinds of life they are expressing. If they enlarge understanding,

42

while understanding need not lead to conduct it may do so. Controversies over whether a work of art is obscene show that the distinction between aesthetic appreciation and moral influence cannot always be sharply drawn. Obscenity, especially pornography, is generally produced for commercial exploitation, and so does not necessarily raise a serious argument about a clash between aesthetic and moral values. But that there can be a clash is shown when it is asked whether a genuine work of art may have a 'tendency to deprave'. 'Tendency to deprave' suggests that showing certain passions and practices in pictures, stories or plays will encourage them. The prosecution would have no case at all unless art can be not only morally expressive, but also morally influential. Admiration, horror, fascination, it can be said, not only move people aesthetically but can also affect their behaviour.

It may well be that to separate moral and aesthetic values, looking on works of art as existing in their own right, 'art for art's sake', only happens in a particular state of society. There have been, and probably still are, societies where the work of art is part of a context with a living moral and religious significance. The setting of the Mass is for celebration, not for performance in a concert hall; the picture is an altar-piece directing devotion; the dance is a ritual one. These contexts are religious, and traditional religion is likely to be a carrier of moral values. Moreover, there is an aesthetic aspect not only in works of art, where it predominates, but as an accompaniment in any number of things: getting a shot just right in a game, cooking and serving a meal, importantly in the fittingness of some imaginative actions. The aesthetic aspect, instead of combining with the other aspects, may then be separated off and be made the purpose of the action and its justification. This is probably only possible in a sophisticated society, where the primary activities are less obviously pressing and where moral forms of justification have become suspect.

At one end of the scale there is the refined aestheticism of people, of whom the late Gilbert Murray was an example, who hesitate to make moral judgements, yet want to commend certain kinds of behaviour. This refined type is likely to talk about 'beauty' rather than aesthetic satisfaction, since this latter may come from spectacles of horror as well as of harmony. Perhaps there is an echo here of the Greek conflation of τὸ κάλον, the beautiful, with τὸ ἀγαθόν, the good. The German

Romantic notion of the *schöne Seele* may express this kind of aestheticism. At a further remove from morality would be the cult of taste and artistic style as being what really matters in the conduct of life. This seems to have been characteristic of the court life of mediaeval Japan, if we can judge from the picture given, for instance, in *The Pillow Book of the Lady Sei Shōnagon*,[1] and it probably needs the circumstances of a leisured society for its cultivation.

There is another end of the scale, where actions are done for aesthetic satisfaction, found in ways which make other people suffer. Aesthetic satisfaction as well as sex can be an element in some forms of sadism. The literature of crime is full of examples of murderers finding satisfaction in exquisitely ingenious murders, though this may be more true of criminals in literature than of actual criminals, who are likely to behave as they do because they have ceased to care morally rather than because they are looking for aesthetic thrills. But criminals apart, the desire to get an aesthetic thrill may be the motive, and the production of aesthetic satisfaction the justification, given for conduct by people who do not want to talk in moral terms. Moreover, there may be an aesthetic fascination in evil, heightened by knowing that it is evil. In the latter case, the fascination would not only be aesthetic, but contain an element of defiance on the part of someone who still recognises good and evil, and wants to show that he is superior to them, as in the 'Satanism' of the nineteenth century Romantics described by Mario Praz in his book *The Romantic Agony*. The 'Evil, be thou my Good' of Milton's Satan is a rebel's 'transvaluation of values', a posture, rather than a position 'beyond good and evil'.

'Good', used to justify an action aesthetically, would mean it gives aesthetic satisfaction. There is a vast literature on aesthetics, and I hope that for my purpose it is sufficient if I say that I take 'aesthetic satisfaction' as being the enjoyment of pure sounds, shapes, smells, or, in the case of constructed works of art, the embodiment of feelings, impressions, thoughts in a physical medium, so that what is expressed and the medium in which it is expressed can be appreciated as fitting each other. This enjoyment need serve no further purpose, though the things in which it is found may serve a purpose. Nor is it a call to action. It may indeed incidentally encourage us to act one way rather than another towards our fellow men—I have said that art need not be morally impotent—but this influence is something over and above the aesthetic pleasure. Justification for aesthetic pleasure might be given by appealing not just to a person's own feeling, but to the verdict of an Ideal Observer, who gives his approvals and disapprovals in aesthetic and not in moral terms (I discuss Ideal Observers in Chapter 12.) An Ideal Observer is said to have detachment; he could only give an aesthetic verdict if as well as this he also had aesthetic interests, though having aesthetic interests would not necessarily give him aesthetic taste. However, my concern here is not with aesthetic standards, but with aesthetic attitudes, and the power to 'distance' oneself attributed to an Ideal Observer might be a component in these.

I have been speaking of aesthetic judgement from the point of view of the spectator. In deciding what to do, an agent might ask himself not only what would satisfy him aesthetically, but he might also see the effort to produce something of aesthetic value—above all some work of art—as having an absolute priority, and his relations with other people as instrumental to this, rather than as important in their own right. Thus Baudelaire could justify behaviour as experience out of which poetry could be made, even when he saw it as sinful (since he kept his Catholic background) and called it 'evil'. But there were flowers of evil—*Les fleurs du mal*. What mattered was to create symbols of beauty out of these —'*tu m'a donné ta boue et j'en ai fait de l'or.*' Rimbaud is another who created poetry out of his experiences of evil as well as of good. But his poetry grew out of a quest which was a religious rather than an aesthetic one. He sought experiences which would unite him with God—indeed make him God—and he was prepared to seek them in the occult. This was followed in the spirit of 'Ye shall be as gods knowing good and evil', and with a freedom which was to be bound by neither. 'We were promised that they would bury in darkness the tree of good and evil, that they would banish tyrannical properties, so that we might bring here our very pure love. It began with some repugnance, and it ends—since we cannot at once grasp this eternity—it ends with a stampede of perfumes'[2] In the end, after great suffering, he made a 'clearance sale' of his illusions.[3] And in *Une saison en enfer* he also acknowledges defeat: 'I, who called myself a seer or an angel, exempt from all morality. I am returned to earth, with a duty to seek, and rugged reality to embrace.'[4] His is the tragedy of a religious quest beyond good and evil, a tragedy out of which a supreme poet created poetry. It is not aestheticism.

The artist's dedication to his art is not itself an aesthetic attitude; indeed, the artist may be struggling to express the truth he sees rather than to get aesthetic experience, which can come afterwards in contemplating the result. His calling as an artist falls within the morality of carrying out a purpose with its own form of internal integrity. It is a moral attitude in which priority is given to following this calling, and this can be at the expense of civic and personal relations. I shall be looking more closely at this as a problem within and not beyond morality in considering how far single-mindedness can be said unreservedly to be a virtue. As a problem within morality, it is other than the question of substituting an aesthetic for a moral justification of actions.

To justify actions aesthetically is not the same as taking up an aesthetic attitude to the world as spectacle, and being reconciled to it on aesthetic but not on moral grounds. This does not exclude a moral attitude in one's dealing with one's fellow men. It may be possible to have this moral attitude, and at the same time to say that aesthetic acceptance is the only bearable metaphysical attitude which one can take without wishful thinking. It may also be possible to say that to cultivate such an attitude can be a way of achieving detachment, and that this can influence one's practical attitudes by freeing them from self-preoccupation.

Schopenhauer is instructive here. His metaphysics is a view of the world seen as an expression of Will—not of will as conscious activity, but as relentless striving, destroying the individual for the sake of the species, and yet canalised in individuals who seek to preserve themselves in ways doomed to frustration. Thus, to live is to suffer. Deliverance can be sought through overcoming self-centredness, in the abnegation of the will, in a state of contemplation to which art gives the entry. The self disappears as a subject which desires and wills, though not as one which is aware, since it seeks to reach a state of pure knowledge, intuiting the Ideas behind phenomena. (Here Schopenhauer is closer to Plato than to Kant.) When the subject abnegates himself as an individual, he can feel his unity with all other life and persons as expressions of the one Will, and therefore as suffering. This feeling is sympathy, for Schopenhauer the only non-possessive, non-destructive kind of love: 'all love which is not sympathy is selfishness.'[5]

There are artists whose vision of some aspect of life is inspired with compassion: a moral feeling though not a moral judgement. Schopenhauer looks to a state of pure contemplation which is even more detached. He speaks indeed of a person in this state as able to do 'the works of love', and it is tempting to think that one might add him as an unexpected witness to the mystics who have found that states of detachment from self issue in love for one's fellows. Moreover, he draws the distinction between love as *agape* and love as *eros* more than a century before Nygren's well-known discussion of their distinction.[6] For Schopenhauer, *agape* is sympathy with universal suffering, and it is in this sense presumably, rather than in a practical and activist sense, that we should take his use of the phrase 'the works of love'. *The Works of Love* is also the title of a book by Kierkegaard, and one wonders whether he could have borrowed it from Schopenhauer. But for Kierkegaard, love means more than sympathy with suffering. Indeed, he asks 'Which of these two loves works more; the happy who sympathizes with another's suffering, or the unhappy who truly sympathizes with another's joy and happiness?' and he answers that it is the latter.[7] Schopenhauer, on the other hand, says that 'Whatever goodness, love and generosity may do for others, it is always done only in alleviation of their sufferings, and therefore that which can move them to good deeds and works of love is always only the knowledge of another's suffering made directly intelligible by reference to, and equated with, one's own'.[8] Such sympathy, in realising one's unity with all suffering, is part of the cure for the illusion of individuality. Is it for Schopenhauer a 'good' state, still more a moral state, or is it a state beyond good and evil?

Schopenhauer is ambiguous about goodness. He speaks of the sympathy felt by the man who has renounced volition as 'good', and indeed as 'the root of morality', but in speaking of practical morality, he says 'good' and 'bad' refer to objects of volition, and so would be left behind with its renunciation. He speaks of social morality in almost Hobbesian terms, as a means of mutual protection to lives and property, and as such belonging to the world which has to be abnegated. The final state is one in which no obligations, no 'oughts' appear. On a wider view of the constituents of morality, seeking this state could be seen as a moral purpose, though attaining it would be to cease to have any purposes. The sympathy which flows from this state could be called a moral rather than an aesthetic feeling, since it is compassion and not contemplative enjoyment. Schopenhauer speaks with approval of the teachings of certain mystical forms of religion, Eastern rather than Christian, which seek to achieve this state. It is a mystical state 'where artists share, in the saintly condition of utter self-forgetfulness, liberation from the Will and pure objective vision', says Erich Heller in *The Ironic German*.[9] The German to whom the title refers is Thomas Mann, who, Heller says, kept returning to Schopenhauer's vision. Mann's novels are preoccupied with the ways in which the artist is cut off from the ordinary goings-on of personal, civic and social life. He saw the temptation to withdraw into art, particularly into music (the art most devoid of moral content) as leading the German intellectual elite to abdicate from concern with problems of civic and political morality. The civic virtue in the Buddenbrooks family declines generation by generation, and in the end they just have their music as a serious interest. And it was for the sake of his music that Levenkühn in Mann's *Dr Faustus* makes his pact with the Devil.

Another great aesthetician, besides Schopenhauer, whose aesthetic attitude becomes ethical in spite of himself, is Nietzsche. The fitting response to the world, at any rate for the early Nietzsche, is one in which it is seen as an aesthetic spectacle, and where moral judgement would be out of place. In *The Birth of Tragedy* he speaks of how the person who can so see the world acquires liberation; and later, in *The Gay Science*,[10] he says, 'As an aesthetic phenomenon existence is still endurable to us, and through art we are given eye and hand and above all a good conscience, to enable us to make of ourselves such a phenomenon.' But besides this, Nietzsche presents a call to superior people to practise heroic virtue. This call puts the person who follows it beyond recognised morality—Nietzsche says 'beyond good and evil', a phrase which he put into currency. Recognised morality for him is a banal Christian morality, the defence of small men against exceptional men: small men in envy passing judgement on great men. In denouncing this, as he does above all in *Antichrist*, he cannot escape from moral tirades, and his attack on the influence of Wagner's music as corrupting is a moral rather than an aesthetic attack. Yet we come back to a fundamental aesthetic verdict, since in the last resort the judgement on the achievement of the superior men is aesthetic —admiration of splendid great men contrasts with disgust at slimy little men. Nevertheless, the superior men themselves are strivers, not aesthetic spectators. They are called to do what will be difficult and exacting, and he speaks as though such costing effort was self-justifying. They have an alternative morality to Christian morality, a form of teleological morality.

Nietzsche thus cannot escape morality. The great anti-moralists like Schopenhauer and Nietzsche are moralists in spite of themselves. Nietzsche's morality of dedication to a creative aim brings out the tension between this and the more deontological morality of transactions between people. Such tension is likely to be a story told especially of artists, since they, more than most others, can claim to be following a creative calling. Also the possibility of creating art—even beauty—out of the sufferings and conflicts of the world can be seen as a way of giving them meaning, and artists may believe that this must be given absolute priority over the claims of personal relations and the morality in these claims.

The young artist, Louis Dubedat, in Shaw's *The Doctor's Dilemma* believes in this absolute priority. He rejects 'morality', but follows the Nietzschean ideal of the artist. When dying, he says, 'I believe in Michael Angelo, Velasquez and Rembrandt, in the might of design, the mystery of colour, the redemption of all things by beauty everlasting, and the message of Art that has made these hands blessed. Amen, Amen.' Dubedat is full of self-deception. He does not acknowledge that he is always scrounging, not only from the doctors who can afford it, but from others who certainly cannot. He speaks of art as the only and final justification, and is convinced of the value of his own work. He does not look at the moral cost; he takes for granted that this must be paid by others.

A non-fictional example is given in Françoise Gilot's *Life with Picasso*. Here Picasso states the moral problem of whether an artist should sacrifice other people for his art; the conclusion is that he should, but this is seen as a problem. 'The sufferings one has inflicted on others, one begins to inflict on oneself equally. It is a question of the recognition of one's destiny and not a matter of unkindness or insensitivity.'[11]

This is not a situation where art replaces morality—the 'destiny' could be to do something other than produce works of art. It is an issue within morality itself, where a person can be seriously asking himself what he ought to do. He is not taking up an aesthetic attitude instead of a moral one, but taking up a particular moral attitude, where justification for his behaviour is given by reference to an ultimate commitment. The analogy is closer to the religious attitude of dedication to a calling than to the spectator-like attitude of aesthetic judgement. (The analogy is with the aesthetic commitment, not with the aesthetic *attitude* to religion, which can be a way of enjoying religious forms of expression without bringing in factors such as belief, penitence, conduct, which normally go with them.)

The morality of the artist in concentrating on his calling is thus a particular case of a morality which gives priority to a single purpose. The person, on the other hand, who adopts an aesthetic attitude to life is not asking what he should do to fulfil his calling as an artist. He is letting aesthetic judgements govern his approvals and disapprovals of conduct, both of his own and of other people. He may be a hedonist seeking pleasure in aesthetic experience. Or, more seriously, he may be transferring the aesthetic acceptance of the world, which can be a deep metaphysical attitude, to an attitude of acceptance in human situations. Such acceptance may be the acceptance of tragedy and this can encompass compassion. Or it may be an acceptance in ironic detachment, seeing the world as comedy, Or it may be an ecstatic acceptance of the passing spectacle. Nietzsche gives this last a metaphysical expression—'my Dionysian world of the eternally self-creating, the eternally self-destroying, this mystery world of the two-fold voluptous delight, my "beyond good and evil," without goal, unless the joy of the circle is itself a goal'[12]—and its religious expression might be one interpretation of the Dance of Shiva. Aesthetic acceptance, whether tragic, comic or ecstatic, is a perennial protest against moralism. But it lacks civic courage, and can ignore a cry for help.

5 Religion within the Bounds of Social Morality[1]

Aesthetic judgement may provide an alternative to moral judgement, both as expressing an attitude towards the world and as appraising human conduct. Can the same be said of religious judgement? A religion is indeed generally assumed to sanction, if not to prescribe, a morality, but the connection may be a contingent and not a necessary one, so that, though religion usually involves morality, it need not do so. If the connection is contingent, then there is the possibility of conflict, and where there is conflict, the question of priority can arise.

I shall start with a view which so defines religion that the connection is necessary, and conflicts of principle between religion and morality, as distinct from conflicts in particular local practices, could not arise.

Kant in *Religion within the Bounds of Mere Reason* saw religion as an expression of reverence for the moral law. Current anthropologists have put this empirically in a way which would have horrified Kant, but with the gain of being able to pay more regard to the varieties of moral law. That religion might be beyond good and evil would therefore seem a strange proposition to most of its contemporary anthropological interpreters, for whom morality is dominant and religion its symbolic expression and reinforcement.

I shall examine this view in some detail, since it can be put with force, and, if correct, it places religion firmly within the bounds of social morality, so that any claim to go beyond good and evil could only arise among religious deviants.

The view can, I have said, be put with some force. For whether we see 'love' as the highest blessing or whether we say 'L'enfer c'est les autres', relations with other people are an inescapable part of life. We have to have ways of behaving towards these others, even if only ways of using them for our purposes. Indeed Hobbes has made a case for saying that social morality is a means of protecting

51

people against each other. Religious demands are then seen as social pressures which induce an individual to accept the moral authority of the group, and which also support him in doing so, moving his imagination by emotionally charged symbols.

This is the view associated with Durkheim, a founding father of sociology. Durkheim, like Edmund Burke, saw societies as cohering and continuing not through conscious planning and direction, but through the working together of a number of different institutional practices, in economic, legal, family, cultural life. But—and this is an important 'but'—these complementary practices do not just work together automatically like parts of a smooth-running machine. The functioning of a society depends on a moral discipline which is not merely prudential, in the sense that people can see that it will be a matter of self-interest to follow it. It is much more a matter of sharing certain deep-seated emotional attitudes of approval and disapproval, and capacities to feel admiration, indignation, disgust at certain kinds of behaviour—the kind of feeling which Burke called 'prejudice', in a non-pejorative sense, where 'prejudice' means an inbuilt response not reached through conscious consideration and argument. Contemporary moralists would call this an 'emotive attitude' view of morality. Durkheim's point is that these attitudes need to be widely shared among members of a society if it is to cohere and continue with any stability; he speaks of them as forming a 'collective conscience' and as 'collective representations'. This language is unfortunate in so far as it suggests that a society is a sort of composite being with a composite mind, but it need not be so taken. The point is that these moral responses are not ideas deliberately thought up by nameable individuals; they are passed on in people's education in school, family life, social intercourse, and above all are expressed in symbolic guises in religious teaching and ritual. Durkheim has been criticised for representing religion and morality as social phenomena; but, as Talcott Parsons remarks[2] it is at least as true to say that he makes society a moral phenomenon.

The belief that a society depends for its existence on intuitively held, widely shared, and emotionally expressed moral reactions has been reiterated by Lord Devlin (fortunately with a lawyer's conciseness instead of a sociologist's diffuseness) in his Maccabean Lecture 'The Enforcement of Morals'.[3] This led to an intermittent controversy on a very high level with Professor Hart.

Professor Hart's main contributions will be found in the three lectures in his book *Law, Liberty and Morality*.[4] Devlin maintains that every society needs to have some emotionally held moral convictions, and that conduct which seriously violates these will be punished by the criminal law, even if such conduct cannot be shown to harm other people in any way other than affronting their moral feelings. However, according to Devlin this latter is not a negligible kind of harm, since, like Durkheim, he holds that the strength of a society will decline if its main moral convictions are weakened. Hart argues against this broadly on J. S. Mill's lines; that, whatever our private moral convictions, the criminal law is only justified in intervening where conduct can be shown to be actually hurtful to other people, and not when it is simply held to be *wrong*. He shows that Devlin is not only saying that the law should take note of certain kinds of conduct because in threatening its moral codes they threaten the security of society (as for instance, treason might be a threat). He is also saying that the criminal law punishes some things because of a conviction that they are wrong. (Blasphemy, and bigamy in a case where the parties might mutually consent, would be examples.)

I think Devlin has the better of the argument in so far as he is giving an account of the actual practices of our criminal law. This does indeed punish certain kinds of conduct because they are held to be wrong in themselves, and not only wrong in virtue of deleterious effects on other people. Criminal punishment has a ritual aspect as an expression of public reprobation, and is not only seen as something to be justified, if at all, on deterrent, utilitarian grounds. This is, in fact, the view behind our criminal law;[5] Hart is asking whether it *ought* to be the view behind it.

Durkheim also held that punishment was a ritual act in which 'Society' expressed its indignation at certain kinds of conduct. Such public expression of indignation, he says, strengthens the public sentiments which have been affronted. The criminal thus unintentionally serves a social function in providing an occasion for this reinforcement of moral emotions—as we might say, '*O felix culpa!*'.

There are several troubles here, including the fact that sadistic emotion as well as moral indignation can get into the demand to see people punished. As a sociological argument of how people regard punishment, it should trouble us because it presupposes a common agreement on fundamental moral convictions, and on

crime as a violation of these. Whatever may be true in very simple
societies, this is certainly not true in a complex society such as our
own, where there may be differences in moral convictions among
different parts of the population. Nor would it hold where a
government is seen as oppressive, so that some 'criminal' acts
might be applauded, and criminals seen as heroes rather than as
reprobates. In such cases their punishment may serve to strengthen emotions at variance with those of the dominant powers in a
society.

This shows that neither Durkheim's view nor Devlin's version
of it gives sufficient weight to the diversity of moral standards in
complex societies, or to the difference of weight people may give to
different considerations in their moral judgements. These writers
stress the public expression of moral sentiments as something in
which nearly everyone except a few 'deviants' can join, and so as a
way of emphasising and reinforcing an underlying harmony. And
Durkheim (though not, as far as I know, Devlin) sees religion as a
symbolic expression of this harmony.

On such a view, the main interest in studying a religion will lie
in observing its *rituals*, rather than expounding its beliefs. These
latter, in myths and dogmas, will be looked on as stories or images
expressing certain fundamental moral values, concerning in particular the proper forms of social relations between people and
groups within the society (including its dead ancestors and its
children yet to be born). They will be seen as *ideological*, i.e. as
ways of thinking justified not as theoretical truth, but as pragmatic means of strengthening a way of life, and rituals will be
occasions when the values which support the fundamental underlying harmony of society are strengthened through symbolic
enactment.

I have said that this view, broadly Durkheim's, stresses harmony rather than conflict, and sees conflicts within a society as
deviations to be brought under control with the help of the ways in
which the dominant social approvals and disapprovals get re-
established in people's minds through emotionally charged symbolic action. Conflicts are seen as aberrations to be corrected and
reconciled, and ritual as one of the main social instruments for
doing this. Hence the tendency in this view to stress ritual as a
means of securing conformity. It may not have been devised for
this purpose by priests and kings anxious to maintain their own
power, as the radicals of the Enlightenment and early nineteenth

century thought. But if not, it serves the purpose even better, since those who officially promote it are caught up in the same ideology as the ordinary participants. There can nevertheless be a confidence trick here if the promoters come to see that what they are doing, ostensibly because of certain beliefs of a 'mystical' kind, has in fact only a pragmatic justification as reinforcing a social way of life.

Some more recent work along these lines goes beyond Durkheim's account, while remaining within his essential method, by fastening on *conflict* as a deep-seated, and not merely ephemeral, aspect of social life. It looks within the symbolism of a ritual for signs of conflicting moral values, not only the moral values of the 'establishment'. It also sees conflict as something to be reconciled if possible, but if not, as something to be contained and lived with.

In particular there is the demand that those taking part together in a ritual of a sacramental kind, such as a sacrifice or a sacrificial meal, should first overcome their grievances with one another. This demand is said to be widespread at any rate throughout Africa. Meyer Fortes writes:[6] 'One cannot sacrifice propitiously with someone who is an enemy. This, according to native theory, would cause the ancestors to become angry, for "as you are towards each other, so are the spirits of your ancestors towards one another".' So the sacrifice in which people eat together 'is both an expression and a pledge of mutual amity and dependence'. The Swiss missionary anthropologist Junod, in *The Life of a South African Tribe* has gone into more detail than this. 'Cultivate good relations', people are told; 'bring everything to the light.' Sometimes angry altercations follow and hold up the sacrifice. Then may come a comic interlude, as when wives run off with the meat of the sacrifice and start eating it in the bush, and have to be chased by people laughing and joking.[7] We see here not only honesty in bringing grievances to light, but also the beneficial effects of a commonly shared joke in reducing the temperature. In the Anglican sacrament of Holy Communion, the invitation to 'draw near' is extended to those who not only truly and earnestly repent of their sins, but are also in love and charity with their neighbours. Unlike the Africans, opportunities for effecting this before the sacrament are not usually produced; this is one of the ways in which the communal significance of religious practices has been watered down. One reason may be that in our larger, more differentiated, society, it is more possible to avoid people

with whom one is not in good will than it is in a small tribal
community. But there are still pockets within our society where
interaction cannot be avoided; where, whatever people's feelings
towards one another may be, they must perforce live and work
together, and some reconciliation procedure, whether formalised
or not, can have a place.

Occasions for the clearing of grievances may not only occur
before public sacrifices or other public rituals. They may also
occur in the context of rituals designed to help a particular person
in a particular affliction. Victor Turner has described one such
ritual—the Ihamba healing ritual among his Ndembu—in considerable detail.[8] In this ritual a doctor extracts a foreign sub-
stance, to wit a tooth, from some part of the body of a sick man.
While he is preparing to do this, the relations and other villagers
cluster round and express concern for the sick man and also bring
out their grievances against him and against each other. The
doctor invites them to come in order of seniority to the hunter's
shrine which has been set up to the shade who is afflicting the
patient, to confess any secret ill-feeling they may have towards
him. Turner writes (op. cit., p. 392):

> It seems that the Ndembu doctor sees his task less as curing
> an individual patient than as remedying the ills of a corporate
> group. The sickness of the patient is merely a sign that some-
> thing is rotten in the corporate body. The patient will not get
> better until all the tensions and aggressions in the group's
> interrelations have been brought to light and exposed to ritual
> treatment. . . . Emotion is roused and then stripped of its illicit
> and antisocial quality, but nothing of its intensity, its quanti-
> tative aspect, has been lost in the transformation. . . . The sick
> individual exposed to this process is reintegrated into his group,
> as step by step its members are reconciled with one another
> in emotionally charged circumstances.

Turner considers that the doctor must have been aware that his
production of the tooth from the patient's body (and indeed it
was a human tooth, no mere baboon's tooth or pig's tooth, as all
those present could testify) was a bit of sleight of hand. But he
thinks the doctor did genuinely believe that he was withdrawing
an influence in some way inimical to his patient, and that this
could only happen as all sources of hostility were brought into the

pen, not only hostilities towards the patient himself, but between all members of the group. And in fact the procedure did seem to have a therapeutic effect. So Turner concludes:

> Ndembu ritual may offer lessons for western clinical practice. For relief might be given to many suffering from neurotic illness if all those involved in their social networks would meet together and publicly confess their ill-will towards the patient and endure in turn the recital of his grudges against them. However, it is likely that nothing less than ritual sanctions for such behaviour and belief in the doctor's mystical powers could bring about such humility and compel people to display charity towards their suffering neighbour (op. cit., p. 393).

This, of course, raises once more the question of whether the effectiveness of such rituals depends on a belief that something more is involved in them than the expression and management of social relations—whatever form this belief in 'something more' may take. Note also that right relationships are sought not just for their own sake, but as a means to another end, in this case the relief of a sick kinsman through the ritual. It might be said that in fact the concern to heal the sufferer simply afforded an occasion for a reconciliation procedure. This would be a case of seeing an incidental socially beneficial result as the primary purpose of the ritual—a tendency to which some functional anthropologists (not Turner) are all too prone. But the reconciliation takes place in a context where there is also another concern—in this case, the healing of the patient. This may be significant: rituals may be more likely to effect reconciliation when they are not exclusively undertaken for that purpose, but where there is some serious common concern for which mutual reconciliation is seen as a necessary condition. Also the ritual is more likely to be a genuine occasion of reconciliation when the participants know each other and interact with each other in other contexts. If they only meet each other in the ritual context, language about mutual reconciliation can hardly be more than a formality.

The conditions for a ritual to be a ritual of reconciliation appear, therefore, to include a wider common concern, realism in diagnosing and acknowledging conflicts, and mutual acceptance of one another, producing readiness to say and to receive what

has to be said—and perhaps, as in Junod's example, resources
of joking behaviour when things get out of hand. But there may be
situations where the structure of social relations will lead to
similar troubles recurring and where, on a longer view, the
ritual will be seen to have been only a palliative. This may well be
the case in some of the witchcraft-cleansing rituals, where the fact
that someone is in a marginal position in the society will lay him or
her open to renewed suspicion when misfortunes occur; or where
some class, women for instance, have to carry responsibilities but
are not given a share in the authority and decision-making of the
society. Or a social arrangement may impose conflicting claims
on people, as assumptions about family obligations and job obligations impose them on many women in our society. In such cases
goodwill engendered in ritual will not meet the problem; what is
needed is a realignment in social relations, and this calls for
rational analysis of the existing set-up and for readiness to change
it.

A social anthropologist may be able to detect some of these
unacknowledged conflicts, expressed in a non-overt way in the
symbolism of a ritual which overtly expresses ideal harmony. He
may do this better if he is aware of a depth-psychological as well
as a social-structural side in the relations between the participants, and if he looks at the symbolism with this double interest.
Turner does this in a paper 'Symbols in Ndembu Ritual'.[9] He
speaks of a 'polarisation of meaning' in ritual symbols. At the
'ideological' pole these refer to moral norms and principles in
social life; at the 'sensory' pole they are associated with natural,
generally physiological, phenomena (such as those connected
with sex, eating, and other bodily processes). These latter can
arouse emotions which are then harnessed in support of the
principles expressed at the ideological pole. 'Norms and values,
on the one hand, become saturated with emotion, while the gross
and base emotions become ennobled through contact with social
values' (op. cit., p. 32). Psycho-analytic interpretations fasten on
the sensory pole, but tend to regard the ideological pole as irrelevant. An example would be boys' initiation rituals. Where these
include circumcision, Freudians see these as expressing the
fathers' jealousy of their sons, and their desire to produce castration
anxiety and make an incest taboo secure. This leaves out the
sociological interest in a *rite de passage* whereby boys are tested
through bearing pain in order to acquire adult stature. If power to

face a new stage of life and new responsibilities is engendered in the ritual, Turner sees it as stemming from the combination of emotion aroused by the 'sensory pole' of the symbols and the ideological values enacted in a drama of social relations. This is, of course, a pragmatic view, in which a ritual and the myths associated with it are seen as instruments for promoting a common social life.

Such a view can take us a long way into the symbolism; far further than the view of ritual as a form of compulsive, and so ineffective, action which Ruth Benedict gave in her article on 'Ritual' in the 1935 *Encyclopaedia of the Social Sciences*. It is instructive to compare this article with the article on 'Ritual' by Edmund Leach in the 1968 *International Encyclopaedia of the Social Sciences*. Leach sees rituals not as compulsive behaviour, but as communication systems within a context of social relations. We have travelled a long way in the thirty-three years between these articles. We shall, however, need to travel further if we are to be prepared to look at why religious rituals seem to need to have a manifest concern with something over and above social relations if they are to have a latent concern with these. It is understandable that social anthropologists should concentrate on the latter, in so far as, by definition, their subject is about social relations, and the socialising effects of religion can be observed in a way that, for example, inner devotion and mystical experience cannot. Nevertheless, if social anthropologists stop at this point, they can be parties to a confidence trick. People who think they know that religion is really a symbol of social morality will be encouraging other people to follow religious practices which they would not want to follow unless they thought that on their inner side they were more than this.

An impressive attempt to hold together the outer social and the inner personal aspects of religion was made by Bergson in his book *Les deux sources de la morale et la religion*.[10]

He did it by speaking not just of aspects but of *sources*. One source is the need for social cohesion; here moral and religious practices are described almost as mechanisms through which a society maintains itself and corrects deviation. This is put in almost pure Durkheimian terms, and it is interesting to note that Bergson and Durkheim were colleagues at the Ecole Normale Supérieure in Paris in their formative years.[11] The pressures of social customs combine with the myth-making power, which he called '*la fonction fabulatrice*', to maintain hope and faith through stories, counteracting the individualistic and possibly disruptive effects of critical intelligence. '*La fonction fabulatrice*' can also serve as a defence against the fear of death and of the natural forces of the environment, by giving these forces a personalised interpretation which brings them closer to human society. But this operation of social custom, even supported by *la fonction fabulatrice*, can lead to stereotypy and lack of adaptability. It will not even maintain itself in a steady state, unless there is some way of infusing new vitality into it. This, Bergson thinks, comes from the influence of people living from the second source of morality and religion, which is a mystical spring. Bergson uses the term 'mystical' widely to refer to a first-hand integral feeling which issues in outgoing love, and which, he believes, is the kind of experience enjoyed by exceptional people—seers, prophets, saints—who are bearers of an 'open' morality and religion, one which can finally extend to humanity, as distinct from the 'closed' type which is limited to a particular social group.

I have not done justice to the persuasiveness of Bergson's vision. But it does leave a number of questions. I shall not go into those connected with the metaphysical background of Bergson's *Creative Evolution*—his view of matter and life. I shall only take it as a view of the relation of morality to religion, where it is surely romantic. Is the 'mystical' feeling expressed by the original person always one of outgoing love? May it not also be daemonic power[12]—which can threaten as well as fertilise social morality? And must social morality, apart from the inspiration and invigoration produced by those exceptional people, just be a matter of mechanical conformity?

There is always a tendency for it to become this. But if this were all, would it even work as social morality—in the crudest terms, as a way of directing behaviour so that a group of people can live together and survive? And if society is to make not just for life but for enhancement of life, as Aristotle and others would say, would such morality produce a way of living in which people could find enough satisfaction to have motives to maintain it? If 'satisfaction' is too general a word, at least there is the fact that people can not only be disciplined into co-operating in various enterprises, but can enjoy doing them, and learn to do them better.

Bergson's mysticism of creative people builds on a view of the social morality of ordinary people as something necessarily unimaginative, and directed to personal or group-protection. Such views of social morality are highly elitist, either explicitly and proudly so, as with Nietzsche, or implicitly, perhaps regretfully so, as with Bergson. I think Bergson would like to say 'Would that all the Lord's people were prophets', but he just cannot believe they will be. Also Bergson does not allow for the fact that some kinds of charismatic prophets see themselves as exempt from normal moral obligations. (Lucian in *De Morte Peregrini* described how wandering prophets used to live on the early Christians, who took them into their homes, and he suggests as the test of a true prophet that he should not stay for more than three days without offering to pay for his meals—coming down to simple social morality with a vengeance.) Thus, while Bergson did indeed write a pioneer essay in which he tried to see religion both as social discipline and as mystical thrust, the connection he gave it with morality turned the social discipline into stereotypy and the mystical thrust into a romantic expansion of love for humanity. If religion in its inner dynamic may not always be so beneficent, then there may be tensions with morality which are not just the tensions between the social *mores* and the moral vision of prophets and reformers. There can be a deeper conflict between morality and the mystical thrust in religion.

In this chapter I have been concentrating on the view of religion as an expression and support for social morality, and have tried to show both why this is a persuasive view, especially to anthropologists, and why, taken as a sufficient view, I think it breaks down as a confidence trick played on those who would not undertake the efforts and commitments involved in religious practices unless they thought they were doing more than this. I have also said that social morality itself may need to be fertilised from a source beyond itself. Yet the action coming from this source can take amoral forms, and the connection of religion with morality has still only been shown to be a contingent one.

6 Religion as the Quest for Powers

The dynamic of religion can supply resources for moral cohesion, for endurance and for reconciliation in situations where, even if we do not find ourselves saying in Auden's words 'We must love one another or die', at least the ability to live and work together may be the price of survival. Yet if religion is not only the drive for social cohesion (as those trying to create civic religions have found to their cost) its relation to social morality is not a necessary one. Nor can morality fertilised from a religious source adequately be reduced to morality symbolised in religious terms. One may go further: there is the possibility that some forms of religion can only reach their goal by leaving morality behind. Not only are they not within the bounds of social morality, but they need to break with them as bonds. Social morality is a stage to be left behind; and in some cases social morality can be seen as society's defence against such forms of religion.

Such a view would be less surprising to an older generation of anthropologists. Older anthropologists started from the association of religion and magic, not of religion and morality. Frazer saw magic as the attempt to exercise powers which were supposed to be efficacious in empirical causality. But they did not work in terms of causality as understood by science (and Frazer in 1890 had no doubt that causality was understood by science). So when people found these techniques did not work, they turned from magic to religion. Religion was a surrender to a supposed power which we cannot use for our purposes. So its essence was resignation, not hope for achieving results. I find a latter-day analogy in the writings on prayer by D. Z. Phillips.[1] Phillips even suggests that to hope that prayers may be answered is superstitious—a view notably different from most sayings on the subject in the Gospels. Few anthropologists would now, I think, go along with Frazer's sharp distinction between magic and religion. They tend to talk about 'magico-religious' practices, a phrase which is noncommittal as to where the one begins and the other ends. In such practices people try to find ways of enhancing their inner powers and to achieve mastery over their circumstances. And in some societies the religious expert, the shaman for instance, is a man who has achieved such powers—in the language of their cosmology, he has become a 'master of the spirits'. Such powers might be capacities to master circumstances through endurance of pain and hardships, or to perform feats as hunters or warriors; or they might be powers of divination, to foresee the future, to diagnose the cause of a disease and find its cure, or to distinguish friends from enemies. If these powers are called 'magical', meaning by this that they are inefficacious, we should not beg the question that they are inefficacious without good empirical reasons. And with the growing body of anecdotal, and sometimes repeatable, evidence of paranormal happenings, we cannot afford to be as dogmatic as Frazer was about what empirically can and cannot happen.

If we look at religion phenomenologically, rather than starting from theological formulations developed within particular traditions, the notion of power or powers would seem to be prior to distinctions of monotheism and polytheism, personal and impersonal, even natural and supernatural.

We may start, then, from men's belief in power or powers operative in their own lives and, they presume, also in nature beyond them. There may be no absolute barriers between the human social world, the animal world, and forces in the physical world. Power may be diffracted into a multitude of powers, perhaps individualised as spirits; indeed the fact that the environment contains forces more likely to be threatening than beneficent may make belief in a plurality of spirits seem more plausible than belief in a single Providence. There may, indeed, also be belief in some hierarchical ordering under a high God—not necessarily, like Chesterton's don, 'remote and ineffectual', as a past generation of anthropologists tended to think, but one whose ministrations, whether beneficent or threatening, came through local agents, whom it may be possible to placate, control, or enlist as protectors. The logical positivist attack on religious propositions, as ostensibly making statements that something is the case which makes no discernible difference to any state of affairs, would surely seem very strange to such believers. They would have no use for gods and spirits who made no difference. A letter

in the Lagos *Daily Times* (c. 1974) advised Nigerians when robbed
or mugged to curse their assailants not by the Christian God, who
doesn't seem to take any action, but by Sango, the Yoruba Thun-
der God, who most surely does.

The notion of powers as individualised in gods and
spirits—'animism' in the jargon— is widespread. But there may
be a still more rudimentary sense of potency not thus individualised—what R. R. Marett called 'pre-animism'. There are a
number of power words—the Melanesian *Mana*, the American
Indian *orenda*, the Arab *baraka*, the Roman *virtus*—all having con-
notations of efficacy which can be possessed by natural objects as
well as by people.[2] 'A thing has *mana*. . . . when it works; it has not
mana when it doesn't work', according to a Fiji islander quoted by
Professor Radin.[3] *Mana* may also mean ritual power attached to
certain statuses, such as those of kings and priests, but its use here
as a prestige word may not be unconnected with its wider use,
since the prestige of certain offices can connect with the belief that
those who hold them are potent in various ways.

Mana may be an exceptional and heightened potency. Beyond
this, there seems to be a more general dynamism—a belief in the
potency of living forces, not distinguished into natural and supernatural. In man, this vital force may be connected with the fact
that his ingestion of food and drink gets turned into energy which
is efficacious in conscious actions—ruling, fighting, and indeed,
just talking. Hence the gods, as well as the ancestors and human
beings, need to be plied with food and drink.

If the development of such powers leads to a state in which, in
the shaman's language, a person becomes 'master of the spirits',
the temptation to use such mastery for one's own purposes rather
than in the service of morally approved social purposes must be a
very present one. We may call it the 'Faustian' temptation. Such
powers, then, are dangerous, both to the individual who possesses
them (or is possessed by them) and to his fellows; so a strong
moral curb may be thought necessary as a protection, and may
call for counter-powers. This, at any rate, seems to be the rule in
societies where the shaman is a servant, while the sorcerer is a
threat, to the community.

Seen anthropologically, therefore, religion shows two aspects;
the support for social morality, and the quest for individual
powers, which may be sought for reasons which need not be
controlled by social morality. A person may be concerned to

achieve and enhance powers by seeking methods which may be empirically efficacious in the outer world, as well as by methods which may lead to mystical development in his inner world.[4] The two may not be unconnected. Powers may be developed in a deliberate attempt at achieving mastery in one's inner world, or inner mastery may be sought as an *askesis* to achieve powers which can be externally efficacious. But there is, I think, a broad distinction between the way of the 'warrior', in which powers are sought, feats accomplished, enemies routed, and the way of the mystic seeking liberation, who may find powers developing unsought. It may even be that one may start from the former aim, and it may turn into the latter. So Lama Anagarika Govinda, in his *Foundations of Tibetan Mysticism* (London, 1959), writing of the Tibetan form of Mahayana Buddhism, says that 'Siddhis', which sound like wonder-working powers but which can be manifestations of the mastery of forces in the psyche, should be looked on as incidental, not to be desired for themselves. 'Whatever is gained by way of miraculous powers loses in the moment of attainment all interest for the adept, because he has grown beyond the worldly aims which made the attainment of powers desirable.' This is illustrated by a story of a robber who submitted to a strict practice of meditation in order to acquire an invincible magic sword, only to find that when he gained it, he did not want it, as the practice of meditation had turned him into a person who no longer desired to be a robber and use such a sword (op. cit., p. 65). This sounds like a religious Catch 22: achieving the means of fulfilling your ambition makes you no longer want to fulfil it. There may, however, be a warning in these stories. The aim to achieve detachment, or liberation, and the aim to achieve Yogic mastery of inner powers can accompany each other, but also cut across each other.[5] Powers are abilities to do something, so there is the question of the end for which they are sought. This may be an enlargement of one's psychic perceptions, for the knowledge this may be hoped to give; it may be in order to meet threats to one's life; it may be to achieve mastery over oneself or over other people. The quest for powers thus raises questions over the morality of one's aims.

The aim may be to achieve inner liberation, and here the development of powers touches mystical development. A proper phenomenology of mystical development must wait for a much more adequate comparative study of different forms of mysticism

than is available at present. I am not competent to make any firm
judgement, for instance, on whether they are all forms with a
single basic pattern. Fortunately for the theme of this book, I can
claim the right to consider them only in so far as they bear on
individual and social morality, and in so far as some of those
following mystical ways say that they reach a stage when they are
beyond good and evil.

In the literature of Eastern Mysticism, whether Buddhist or
Hindu, there are many passages in which social morality is said to
be part of the world of illusory appearances, and the distinction of
good and evil is said no longer to apply within the enlightened
state. In Hinduism there is a widespread practice of carrying out
one's social role, marrying and raising a family, and then withdrawing from the world, and it is said that in this latter stage of
Vanaprastha the moral distinctions proper to the earlier stage will
be left behind.

Professor Zaehner, in his posthumous book *Our Savage God*
(London 1974), collects a number of passages in which good and
evil becomes indifferent, and says that if one follows the implications of such amorality the end-state can be that of Charles
Manson, who is said to have approached the murders of Sharon
Tate and her companions in a state of mystical ecstasy. Zaehner
was conflating a number of forms of mysticism in which there is
said to be a state in which the distinction between good and evil,
right and wrong, is left behind. But this does not make them all
amoral, or at least amoral in the same sense, nor does it mean that
when this state is reached everything is permitted. In Buddhist
forms, the final goal is liberation from desire, and to reach it one
must follow a way of moral discipline in which one becomes free
from ambitions, envy, anger, hatred. These are disturbing emotions, but they are also sources of wrong action. The Dharma is a
way of right living in which these emotions are replaced by
gentleness and forbearance. Distinctions of good and evil in social
action can be said to be superseded as elements in the phenomenal
world from which one seeks to be liberated. But the liberated state
is reached by overcoming the desires which lead to wrong thinking in that world. It can finally become a state in which an
enlightened one manifests the great uncaused compassion. This
can be compared with the language about outgoing love in forms
of Christian mysticism, where although the contemplative may
not talk about right and wrong, there has been moral training in
which he has built up an inner discipline through life with other

people (even hermits were not always hermits, and they could be visited). 'Love and do what you like' may mean for such a one that he has reached a stage in which he can act with acquired moral wisdom, especially where he may break a generally accepted moral rule. There may be a state beyond being deontologically bound by rules where a person is free from anxieties and acquires wisdom about the right thing to do. But if there is a moral discipline behind this state, it is a state in which there is still a concern that right should be done, not a state in which everything is permitted. To be beyond moralism is not to be beyond good and evil.

Dr Irmgard Schloegl, writing about the Zen Buddhist training in 'gentling the bull' within a man,[6] says the transformed man who 'comes back to the market with bliss-bestowing hands',

> is neither bound by morals, nor beyond them, for he has broken into the place from which all morality arises, and is genuinely and naturally 'good', that is, both loving and wise. This also means that he is not blind, that he sees differences very clearly and distinguishes between Buddha and Mara, good and evil, recognizing them when he sees them, they no longer have power over him. They cannot carry him away. Thus he is naturally good.

I should want to say that, besides this mystical source of morality, there is another source in people's ways of managing their social relationships (and therefore, with the qualifications I have already mentioned, I should subscribe to Bergson's view of 'two sources'). Moreover, I do not think that the 'transformed' man is released from the need to *think* about what would be the right thing to do in problematic situations, especially where one takes a complex view of what may constitute moral considerations, though he may bring what I shall try to describe as 'liberty of spirit' to bear in his judgements about them. But my concern here is with how one should take the ostensibly non-moral sayings in some of these forms of religion, where, when 'morality' is said to be superseded, this in effect can mean that one's ideas of good and evil are no longer being taken from the *mores* of the society.

It may still be the case, however, that the moral discipline which is seen as a necessary element in the training for enlightenment, purification, mystical union, is also a means to liberation. Behaviour towards others which results from ambition, envy, anger, will disturb this end. This would be a form of teleological morality in which right actions are those directed towards a goal of liberation. There may however be forms—particularly that of Mahayana Buddhism—where the end includes concern for the liberation of other beings, and is an attainment of enlightenment which works towards this. Anagarika Govinda, in the book *Foundations of Tibetan Mysticism* to which I have already referred, invokes the image of a prism (op. cit., p. 115) to speak of the forms in which the Dhyani-Buddhas (enlightened Radiating Ones) appear in inner vision. He compares these forms with the different colours into which the rays of the sun are separated, when passing through a prism, thus revealing in each colour a particular quality of the light. Since he has used this image of a prism, I shall compare his use of it with mine, in particular in its relevance for morality. Govinda connects it with the colour symbolism in the doctrine. The prism image (which is of course Govinda's, not traditional Buddhist) is combined with colour symbolism. There are three colours into which the total meditative vision is split so as to be apprehensible to the human mind—the yellow of the Wisdom of Equality, which is a pure feeling for all beings; the red of the Discriminating Wisdom; the green of the All-Accomplishing Wisdom through which Enlightenment passes into action. The white of the Mirror-like Wisdom reflects in outer forms the undifferentiated total wisdom, the blue of the dazzling dark of consciousness. (Here the prism image is left behind.)

There is difference as well as analogy between Govinda's use of the image and my own. I have used it to suggest how the white light of pure moral judgement gets refracted into a spectrum of different considerations to which attention is directed in trying to decide what to do, and it may fasten on one of these. A Buddhist might say that I am talking about making moral judgements in the world of 'Maya', not about right actions issuing from enlightened wisdom. I think that the Buddhists are right in seeking to cultivate an intuitive wisdom which can be brought to bear in judgements of what is right, and I shall try in my last chapters to say something about how I see moral judgement as having a mystical source as well as sources in reason and in customary *mores*. But I shall still be stressing the complexity and problematic character of moral conflicts. The Buddhists teaching is fastening on the factor of acquired intuitive wisdom, and I am impressed by the way in which this also is described as having complexity as well as simplicity, showing itself in different aspects. The Dhyani-Buddha might manifest red of the Discriminating Wisdom or the green of All-Accomplishing Wisdom. So the mystical source itself is not just an undifferentiated feeling; it is shown in a range of different qualities. Among these, those symbolised by the yellow and green colours directly express a non-self-seeking concern for others; this form of mystical development certainly contains its moral ingredient, both in the process by which it is attained and the attitude to which it leads.[7]

There may, however, be forms of mystical development where the emphasis is on the quest for powers rather than on enlightening wisdom, and where the moral ingredient is less apparent. This may well be true of the left-handed Tantra, where the aim is the liberation and enhancement of powers through practices which break away from the restrictions and taboos of social morality. But even here, there is some ritualised form in which these practices are contained (for instance in the teaching about withdrawal in ritualised sexual practices).

The mainstream religions are concerned with bringing powers released in mystical exercises into relation with social morality, so that their potential dangers can be controlled. The witch doctor, the medicine man, the shaman may become 'masters of the spirits', but they are also servants of their community. The witch and the sorcerer also seek powers, but for other ends. The concern to bring these powers within the orbit of social morality may give plausibility to the anthropological view that religions are symbolic forms of social morality; but that such powers need to be channelled shows that they are not just forms of social morality, and can be sought without regard to it.

This seems to be what is happening in the contemporary 'counter-culture'. There is interest in what is called 'altered states of consciousness'—either through meditative exercises, drugs or both, entering into states of mind in which the world is seen differently, different ranges of 'reality' (probably of inner psychical reality) are experienced, and psychic powers released. These states are sought often at considerable personal risk and cost. They can be sought by breaking down inhibitions. Social morality can be seen as one of the inhibitions to be broken down, or as part of the 'establishment' to be resisted. An instance was given in *The Times* of 30 May 1975, reporting that Bill Dwyer was goaled for disobeying an injunction for which he had signed an affidavit not to organise a Pop Festival in Windsor Great Park. He is reported as saying 'I know that I am under an injunction not to organize this festival. But the God I believe in, namely love, has laid on me an injunction to go ahead'. Many religious conscientious objectors down the ages have disobeyed injunctions. What is noteworthy here is that Bill Dwyer had signed an affidavit which he felt free to disregard. He was not concerned either with a deontological regard for keeping one's word, or with the implications for a social way of life of a breakdown of trust in such undertakings, and how such a breakdown might bring an increase in repressive measures.

The widespread interest in Castaneda's books[8] is instructive whatever the truth about their basis in fact. To begin with, Castaneda's Mexican Indian teacher is called a Yacqui *sorcerer*. Castaneda, as a member of a department of anthropology, surely knows that 'sorcerer' is a name generally given to anti-social masters of mystical powers; he does not find it necessary to say that Don Juan was not a sorcerer in this sense. This in itself shows the lack of interest in social morality. Don Juan is not described as a member of any social group—he seems to be a solitary practitioner except for a few individual confederates. His shaman-like activities are not represented as rooted in any indigenous religion, though they may have grown up in one in the past. They are now seen as techniques for a certain kind of mastery. Castaneda's apprenticeship—undertaken clearly at great personal risk—was devoted to learning these powers, so that he himself could graduate as a sorcerer, and could look forward in the end to becoming a 'man of knowledge'. In the fourth of the books, *Tales of Power* (note the title) Castaneda finally learns to follow the 'way of the warrior'. 'A warrior cannot complain or regret anything. His life is an endless challenge, and challenges cannot possibly be good or bad. Challenges are simply challenges . . . in the doings and not doings of warriors, personal power is the only thing that matters' (p. 108).

What matters, then, is to learn the hard way how to achieve this power. At the end of *Tales of Power* there is one hint that there may be a kind of devotion as well as mastery in this exercise. When Castaneda achieves his mastery, and Don Juan leaves him, he is told to fall down and salute the earth. The warrior has come to *love the earth*. 'Only the love for this splendorous being can give freedom to a warrior's spirit; and freedom is joy, efficiency, and abandon in the face of any odds' (p. 286). 'Only if one loves this earth with unbending passion can one release one's sadness', Don Juan says. 'A warrior is always joyful because love is unalterable and his beloved, the earth, embraces him and bestows upon him inconceivable gifts' (p. 285). We end with a nature mysticism which by-passes social morality, yet gives the 'warrior' love and a sense of gratitude towards the earth.

In Castaneda's first book, *The Teachings of Don Juan*, there is indeed a passage which, whatever the truth about Don Juan, is a great piece of spiritual teaching.[9] It concerns 'the four enemies of the man of knowledge'. The first enemy is *fear*. If one succumbs to it 'he will never become a man of knowledge. He will perhaps be a bully or a harmless, scared man; at any rate, he will be a defeated man.' The second enemy is *to believe one has certainty*. 'That *clarity* of mind, which is so hard to obtain, dispels fear, but also blinds.' The third enemy is *power*. 'He will know at this point that the power he has been pursuing for so long is finally his', and he may become cruel and capricious in its use, losing control of himself. The fourth and last enemy is *old age*:

> The one he won't be able to defeat completely, but only fight away. This is the time when a man has no more fears, no more impatient clarity of mind—a time when all his power is in check, but also the time when he has an unyielding desire to rest. If he gives in totally to his desire to lie down and forget, if he soothes himself in tiredness, he will have lost his last round, and his enemy will cut him down into a feeble old creature. His desire to retreat will overcome all his clarity, his power, and his knowledge. But if the man sloughs off his tiredness, and lives his fate through, he can be called a man of knowledge, if only for the brief moment when he succeeds in fighting off his last, invincible enemy. That moment of clarity, power, and knowledge is enough.

Don Juan's teachings are concerned with an ascetic discipline in becoming a 'man of knowledge'; whether or not it be called 'religious', it is a form of spiritual training. As the books go on, the emphasis shifts from the man of knowledge to the man of power, following the way of the warrior, where a 'warrior' is dedicated to 'stalking his weaknesses', and to overcoming obstacles against 'seeing'. In the first book, Don Juan spoke of finding a 'way with a heart', by which he appeared to mean a path on which one finds one can travel joyfully in one's own development, not one which leads to compassion to other people. There is one passage in *The Second Ring of Power* in which Castaneda tells how he gave a lift in his car to a woman with a small boy whom he saw waiting on a bench and wanting to get to the hospital. He recalls how when he asked Don Juan how he could repay him for his help, Don Juan said he could pay something to the spirit of man. But this is an isolated incident, and the act of kindness (though it did also involve a payment at the hospital) was not a very exacting one. The warrior's internal morality, his 'impeccability', consists in finding sureness in the steps he should take to follow his path. Morality towards others consists in being ready to press and challenge them so that they may develop their own power. The warning against the temptation to use power to dominate others still stands.

There may be quests for power in which this does not stand. Power may be sought in a Faustian spirit, in which there is not only lack of interest in social morality, but its repudiation as a hindrance. The person developing power may not recognise restraints on what he is entitled to do in following his aim, whether this be knowledge or self-mastery or some other form of achievement. There is a name for this type, the 'daemonic', a spiritual type which claims to be beyond good and evil, and to this I shall now turn.

7 The Daemonic 'Beyond Good and Evil'

The notion of the Daemonic goes back a long way. It appears in an ancient Greek context, and its history there is interesting as a background to its later fortunes. It stands for a kind of power not necessarily individualised, still less personalised.[1] It is often referred to impersonally: τὸ δαιμόνιον. H. J. Rose[2] thinks a daemon may have first been a spirit, and then been thought of impersonally. E. R. Dodds says:[3] 'Such evidence as we have suggests rather that while μοῖρα developed from an impersonal "portion" into a personal Fate, δαίμων evolved in the opposite direction, from a personal "Apportioner", cf. δαίω, δαιμόνη, to an impersonal "luck". There is a point where the two developments cross and the words are virtually synonymous.' It can also be used adjectivally of someone or something that manifests power. In addressing a person, ὦ δαιμόνιε is like 'Your Excellency', but sometimes also it is less respectful and more convivial—rather like 'my good Sir'. ἀγαθός δαίμων is also used as a toast—'Here's luck'. In some of these forms of address it is not so much a status word as a property word for someone or something having some special powers, which are not quite divine but can be somehow connected with divinity. There is the connotation with powers to assign, especially to assign one's path in life. In the Myth of Er in the *Republic* (620e), when the souls have chosen the life they are going to lead on earth, each one is assigned his daemon.

The most famous of all daemons of Greek antiquity was, of course, the daemon of Socrates. According to Socrates' testimony, as Plato gives it, especially in the *Apology* and *Phaedo*, it was an inner monitor which warned him when he was betraying his vocation. It was the God, Apollo, who assigned the vocation; and the daemon does not tell Socrates what to do, but warns him when he is doing something contrary to it. Plutarch has a discussion of this in a comparative religious vein in *De Genio Socratis* (περὶ τοῦ

Σωκράτους δαιμόνιον). There is a suggestion that the sign was a
sneeze. A sneeze could be a disturbance of the life spirit—which
is why people used to say 'God bless you!' to avert a potential
danger (not just the danger of catching someone's cold). The
Romans said *'Salve'*. The suggestion that it was a sneeze is
rejected, and the kind of experience it may have been is compared
and contrasted with the experiences reported by Timarchus, a
young philosopher, who gets psychedelic visions in the crypt of
the oracle Trophomius, where he sees shooting stars which he is
told are daemons of exceptional men. Socrates' inner admonitory
voice, on the other hand, was said to come when he was quiet, not
in a dream or passion. He was able to go into trances, or at any
rate, into periods of intense abstracted concentration—Alcibiades
describes in the *Symposium* how he stood like this through a whole
night while on a campaign—but these were not the experiences he
interpreted as coming from his daemon. These latter were audit-
ory not visionary, and directly connected with warnings if he were
not keeping to his vocation as a philosopher.

Socrates' daemon seems to have been a philosopher's version of
the notion of the daemon as a guardian spirit. A daemon can be an
inspirational power, not only, as with Socrates, an admonitory
one. Daemons are said to guide inspired men, seers and prophets.
But there can also be an evil daemon, κακὸς δαίμων, a deceiver
or bringer of ill luck. Xerxes in the *Persae* is tempted by an evil
daemon. But Aeschylus makes Darius' ghost say that the disaster
to the Persian fleet was punishment for his pride, *hybris*, and that
νόσος φρενῶν—a disease of the mind—had possessed him
(*Persae*, 750).

To connect psychological states and cosmological powers was
characteristic of the Greek tragedians. They (especially
Euripides) come close to the point of giving a psychological
interpretation. But these psychological forces are also seen as
cosmic forces, or as swayed by cosmic forces, and it is in this
sphere, where the psychological and the divine meet, that the
Greek notion of the daemonic lives. Since divinity for the Greeks is
not necessarily good, at least in any ordinary moral sense, the
daemonic need not be a power for good. But it is a power, and can
be a charismatic one.

Since personal and impersonal interpretations get inter-
changed and cross over into each other, τὸ δαιμόνιον, 'the
daemonic' can become ὁ δαίμων—a particular daemon—and

then again lose its identity. It can be seen as an external power invading a person and possessing him, to do things for good and ill which are not according to his own deliberate intention. Or it can be seen as a deep part of his own psyche. $\mathring{\eta}\theta o\varsigma$ $\mathring{\alpha}\nu\theta\rho\acute{\omega}\pi\omega$ $\delta\alpha\acute{\iota}\mu\omega\nu$—'a man's character is his daemon', a saying attributed to Heraclitus—is perhaps the most striking statement of this. We only have the saying as a fragment, and what it means is largely guesswork. Even if it sounds like a psychological interpretation, the connection with a person's destiny is still suggested. For better or worse, what one can do or be stems from character. And what is 'ethos'? Is it just a set of habits, or a deep-seated bent and style of the personality?

The same internal/external and impersonal/personal criss-crossing of interpretations comes out in the Latin rendering of daemon, generally *genius* (not *numen*, the word for divine power, from which 'numinous' is derived). The *genius* may belong to a family or a place—*genius loci*, put personally, is a place's tutelary deity: put impersonally, it is what might be called its 'aura'. Of a person, it can be a guardian spirit, or, impersonally, a dynamic power, associated with creativity though not necessarily, as in English usage, with very high creativity. The etymology is instructive—it is said to be connected with *gigno* 'I grow'. So 'genius' could be a sort of vitalistic notion, of what makes things happen, we might say 'tick'. This etymology excited Jeremy Bentham. He tells us that at the age of twenty, when reading Helvetius, he saw 'genius' could be etymologically connected via *gigno*, with the notion of production or invention, and asked himself 'Have I a genius for anything? What can I produce?' That was the first enquiry he made of himself. Then came another, 'What of all earthly pursuits is the most important?' Legislation was the answer Helvetius gave.... 'Have I a genius for legisla-tion?... I gave myself the answer, fearfully and trembl-ingly—Yes.'[4] And from this point he never looked back.

The daemons went down in the world in early Christian times, though the Latin *genius* retained a good meaning,[5] and in Greek the word $\pi\nu\epsilon\widehat{\upsilon}\mu\alpha$ (*pneuma*) took over some of the sense of a power which could be either part of the psyche, or invade and possess it. But if the pagan gods were not just to be dismissed as illusions, there was the question of what they were. So the combination of good and evil in the daemonic gets split. The good tutelary part gets assigned to the notion of the guardian angel; the rest becomes an evil spirit, and turns into a demon. The demons are then particular evil supernatural powers. They can tempt and torment, but they have lost the dynamic creativity which was the quality of the daemonic.

We have to wait a long time until the daemon begins to come up again the world. It comes up in Germany, particularly in Goethe and Nietzsche, and there the dominant notion is creativity beyond good and evil, so bringing the tension with morality into the centre of the picture.

Goethe is too great a figure only to be a prophet of daemonic creativity. Ideally, he looked for creativity from living close to the springs of life in nature. But nature was not only harmony, vitality, joy. There is a more disturbing character in it.

> He thought he could detect in nature—both animate and inanimate, with soul or without soul—something which manifests itself only in contradictions, and which, therefore, could not be comprehended under any idea, still less under one word. It was not godlike, for it seemed unreasonable; not human, for it had no understanding; nor devilish, for it was beneficent; not angelic, for it often betrayed a malicious pleasure. It resembled chance, for it evolved no consequences: it was like Providence, for it hinted at connection. All that limits us it seemed to penetrate; it seemed to sport at will with the necessary elements of our existence; it contracted time and expanded space. In the impossible alone did it appear to find pleasure, while it rejected the possible with contempt.
>
> To this principle, which seemed to come in between all other principles to separate them, and yet to link them together, I gave the name of Demoniac, after the example of the ancients, and of those who, at any rate, had perceptions of the same kind.
>
> . . . .
>
> Although this demoniacal element can manifest itself in all corporeal and incorporeal things, and even expresses itself most distinctly in animals, yet with man especially has it a most wonderful connection, forming in him a power, which, if it be not opposed to the moral order of the world, nevertheless does often so cross it that one may be regarded as the warp and the other as the woof.
>
> For the phenomena to which it gives rise, there are innumerable names; for all philosophies and religions have tried in

prose and poetry to solve this enigma and to read once for all the riddle, an employment which they are welcome to continue.

But the most fearful manifestation of the demoniacal is, when it is seen predominating in some individual character. During my life I have observed several instances of this, either more closely or remotely. Such persons are not always the most eminent men, either morally or intellectually; and it is seldom that they recommend themselves to our affections by goodness of heart: a tremendous energy seems to be seated in them; and they exercise a wonderful power over all creatures, and even over the elements; and, indeed, who shall say how much farther such influence may extend? All the moral powers combined are of no avail against them: in vain does the more enlightened portion of mankind attempt to throw suspicion upon them as deceived if not deceivers—the mass is still drawn on by them.

Seldom, if ever, do the great men of an age find their equals among their contemporaries, and they are to be overcome by nothing but by the universe itself; and it is from observation of this fact that the strange but most striking proverb must have arisen. *Nemo contra Deum nisi Deus ipse.*[6]

ere is a less dark passage in *Egmont* (Act II) when we have the tion of creative powers driving the individual to a destiny yond his knowledge.

Egmont: Our destiny is like the sun; invisible spirits whip up time's swift horses, away with its light chariot they run, and all we can do is to take the reins with a firm grip, and keep the wheels clear of the rocks on one hand, the precipice on the other. Where we are going, who can tell? We scarcely know from whence we came.

Secretary: My lord, my lord!

Goethe's creative man is pulled in two directions. Professor Erich Heller writes: 'Of these two strivings the one desires the attainment of the superman, the alchemist heightening of all human faculties, whereas the other aims at renunciation and resignation to the simple state of man'.[7] Also Goethe is aware of the pull of social morality. To quote Heller again,

Thus the meaning of creative genius as well as the meaning of doing the sober work of the day, inwardness as well as action, had to remain puzzles to each other, anonymous, undefined strangers. They never met in a common dedication and could not be at peace with each other because they knew no will other than their own and at such a distance from '*la sua voluntate è nostra pace*' neither divine comedy nor human tragedy can be written. It was impossible for Goethe to accept this situation, and impossible, by the very nature of things, to solve it. Hence his perpetual oscillation between the precarious magic of inner communion with the deep where the Earth Spirit dwells, and the moral determination to reconcile himself to the cruder demands made on human existence by society, with the emphasis of approval shifting between the two.[8]

Those, both Greek and German, who have written about the daemonic have been drawn to talk about it not just in psychological and sociological terms, but in mythological and metaphysical ones, where a drive coming from the deep self acquires cosmic overtones. Whatever we make of the metaphysics, this suggests at least that it is not just a manifestation of physical vitality. So I question Goethe's saying that it expresses itself most distinctly in *animals*.

Rollo May in *Love and Will*[9] has one of the few recent discussions of the daemonic, from the point of view of an existentially-minded psycho-analyst. He says it is 'any natural function which has the power to take over the whole organism'; he gives sex and anger as examples, and calls it the power of nature beyond good and evil, both creative and destructive. But I do not think it is just a 'natural function' taking control of the organism. It is a manifestation of what, for want of a better word, we can call a 'spiritual' capacity of the person (though, indeed, like all his capacities, no doubt it has biological roots). It is a quality of *will* in a person who has a drive towards some achievement, and who is imperiously seeking the power to do it, at whatever cost to himself and others. This is a distinctively *human* capacity.

I do not want to put this dualistically, saying man has a spirit as well as a body. I want rather to say that in man vital energies can lead into spiritual capacities. So the vital energy of the daemonic person is not just a biological drive—it is this, but it has also the qualities we describe in terms such as 'will to power' combined with 'creative drive', 'charismatic appeal', and though no one of these defines the daemonic, they can be ingredients in it.

Nietzsche is a prophet of this genre.[10] There are other minor prophets, notably Hermann Hesse, who is widely read nowadays. Hesse wrote mainly in the 1920s, and he had a *'Götterdäm-merung'* approach to the expected war. He hoped it might destroy the old society and make room for the new, which would realise itself through a few chosen individuals. These would follow a religion which embraced both good and evil, not just a truncated good, and they would bear the mark of Cain, taking on themselves what the world called sin in order to be true to their deepest impulses. This truth to oneself is 'the bird coming out of the egg', the new life, contrasted with the restrictions and pulls to conformity in existing moralised cults. Its god would unite the divine and diabolical as they were united in some ancient magical cults, and Hesse calls this god Abraxas, a name used in the formulae of old Greek charms. (I am here mainly following what he says in *Damien*.)

I do not know how influential Hesse was between the wars; he certainly seems to have impressed Jung. At any rate, Abraxas makes his appearance in Jung's *'Seven Sermons to the Dead'*, said to have been written by Basilides in Alexandria, where East touches West, though actually, of course, written by Jung about 1925. The metaphysical background of the world is the 'Pleroma', a 'Nothingness' out of which everything comes. 'Nothingness', however, seems to have fairly positive properties—a way of talking which would surely have called down the curses of the ancient Parmenides against those who try to say that 'not-being is'. It manifests itself in pairs of opposites—Light and Dark, Good and Evil—which we try to establish as separate qualities. 'God' is a first distinction we make, and he is contrasted with 'the Devil'. Behind God and Devil is Abraxas, the effective power of the Pleroma. Man creates the multiplicity of gods and daemons which appear in imagery. But in his inmost life man is also Abraxas, the original creator and destroyer, uniting the opposites of good and evil, and he prays to this God behind God.

I see echoes of this in Jung's remarkable paper on conscience.[11] Jung contrasts his view of conscience with that of the Super-Ego—the built-in inhibitor of actions disapproved of and punished by the parents and others who socialised us. That the Super-Ego is a psychological fact I think practically no one would deny, and Jung does not deny it. The question is whether this is the whole of conscience. For Jung, what might be called the authentic conscience is not the Super-Ego, but the meeting of the conscious mind with original creative power which stems from the unconscious and expresses itself through the archetypes. This means that the archetypes must be thought of as symbolic expressions of original powers in the psyche, not as archaic vestiges of past social conditioning. Whatever status one gives the 'archetypes', note that Jung believes that there is an original creative power of the psyche stemming from the unconscious; it differs from the Freudian instinctual energy of the *id* in being more of a unity, a deep self behind the conscious self which is trying to grow, and which sometimes seems like the power of another person, so getting symbolised as a guardian spirit or inner God.[12] In the chapter on 'The Development of Personality' at the end of *The Integration of the Personality* (London, 1940), Jung speaks of the individual's vocation as an 'inner voice' which calls him away from the inertia of mass conformity—an inner daemon, both creative and dangerous. A person's 'vocation' is found in living not only with but from this deepest self. For our present concern, the important thing is that it is both creative and *morally ambivalent*, as the god Abraxas is prior to the distinction of Good and Evil. And for Jung, this Abraxas-conscience has a religious feel, the collision of consciousness with power (he calls it *mana*) coming from the unconscious and expressed in a numinous archetype. In *Answer to Job*, Jung says the original God is unconscious, combining good and evil. The Christian story is that of this primordial God seeking consciousness in the incarnated God in Christ, in whom good can triumph. But the evil is there split off, so that the Christian God is never the final God behind God, the source of creative energy, and man has to integrate the dark power within him.

For Jung, religion is concerned with this creativity from the unconscious which combines opposites of good and evil. The unity of good and evil in the archetypal experience can, however, be broken—we can try to follow a separated good, or, more significantly, the unintegrated evil can be experienced as another kind of self within the self—in extreme cases as diabolic possession, more generally as what Jung calls 'the Shadow', the dark side of the self which has not achieved its union with the other side and which can be a person's own particular devil.

There is a powerful mystical tradition behind this, going back among the Germans at least to Eckhart, and more explicitly to Jakob Boehme. The picture seems to be that of the psyche rooted in some 'ground of being' which is a non-moral source of creative power. There is then the world of morality, of rights and obligations, where people are conditioned to live socially. Beyond this, there is the possibility for the spiritually gifted individual of surmounting this world of social morality and living from the original springs of his being, in a way that will carry him beyond good and evil.[13] This is seen as a religious way: 'religious', because it stands for a person's ultimate dedication, and also because, even when it is described psychologically, it acquires cosmic overtones. Those who write about it talk of a person following his 'fate' or his 'destiny'. Its centre is the will of an individual, directed towards an aim, which possesses him, and which must be followed at all costs.

Whatever the daemonic person may be striving for, he thus lives from a drive which is exacting in its demands both on himself and other people. Morality appears, if it does, as the call to follow his inner drive wherever it may lead, and the claims of social morality can be seen as at best a distraction, and at worst a pressure to conformity to be resisted.

The Greeks had a strong sense of the dangers of πλεονεξία—going too far—and of ὕβρις—over-confident pride—so that they were never, I think, able to press the demand of the daemonic at all costs in the spirit of the Germans. As a demand which can override human relations, this can be a driving force in the lives of certain great artists (though many artists, as well as scientists, are humble about their work), and also in certain extreme forms of religion: Ibsen's Brand, half daemonic, half potential saint, is an example.

The daemonic person has an overriding aim, and in so far as it is a specific one he exhibits an A type of teleology. A-type teleology need not be exhibited daemonically. It can be a sober form of Utilitarianism, directed to maximising whatever a person sets as his chief value. The daemonic man is not a rational maximiser. He sees his aim as something which possesses him; not so much something chosen as something which impels. Thus he may speak of it in terms such as 'destiny' which have metaphysical or religious overtones. This is something to which I shall return in my last chapter; here I am concerned with the moral aspect, and the daemonic man's claim that he follows a call that takes him beyond good and evil. Whatever else he means by this, he means that it takes him beyond social morality.

The daemonic person draws on energies coming from a deep level of the personality and canalised in a concentration of will which gives him courage, tenacity, endurance. This concentration is more than an assertion of self-will, since he can be possessed by devotion to some cause, or a call to some supreme effort. But he has not achieved the liberty of spirit or detachment from self which could make him sensitive to where self-assertion may be infecting dedication. He may not simply be moved by a will to power as personal ambition, but he may have developed spiritual and even psychic capacities which will give him charismatic power through which he can dominate other people, making them serve his own single-track concern. His lack of any sense of moral complexity may give him strength, but can also lead to his becoming a fanatic or a destructive force. He claims to be beyond good and evil; we might say rather than his narrow concentration of vision fastens on one colour only in the spectrum seen through the moral prism, and that a strident red. He lacks the corrective which might come from looking at the colours which show the needs and interests of others.

There is another, a religious, corrective against self-assertion, which can come from putting a final question mark against one's concern, however imperious, by subjecting it to 'the Will of God'. Can this be a source of *moral* criticism and correction—we might say, can it be thought of as a reference to the unseen white light of an ideal morality, contrasted with the light as we see it, refracted by our moral prism? Or can it also, like the notion of the daemonic, be invoked in a claim to supersede morality?

8 'The Will of God'[1]

'Doing the will of God', or seeking to do it, is a notion close to the centre of, at any rate, Christian, Jewish and Moslem religion. So too is the notion of accepting happenings as God's Will—*Fiat voluntas tua*. In the latter notion, God's Will is something to be accepted rather than accomplished. Where the Will of God is something to be sought and accomplished, then it may be given as a final reason for doing what is believed to be in accord with it. Is it then connected necessarily or contingently with morality? If necessarily, then what is added to 'This is right' by saying 'This is the Will of God', at least as far as the content of the action goes? If the connection is contingent, then the moral judgement that this is right could conflict with the religious judgement that this is in accordance with the Will of God, and if both can be given as finalising reasons we could be faced with two conflicting ultimate demands. If there is a divergence, and the moral demand is said to be subordinate to the religious demand, this would be a claim that religion should in such cases supersede morality.

One answer might be that the two demands could initially diverge because morally I say that I ought to do what I believe to be right, i.e. my 'subjective duty'. The Will of God, it may be said, coincides with what is objectively right. If there is some signalling system whose reliability I can accept by which I can be shown what this is, and how it corrects my own subjective opinions as to what is right, then it would bring the religious demand within what is required by the moral demand. I ought not just to be complacent about my own opinions, but to take any means I can to improve them, so as to close the gap between what I think is right and what really is right, and if information about the Will of God helps me to close this gap, then I should take it, and I would still be making a moral judgement. I must of course, be able to accept the reliability of the signalling system and believe that what God wills is right. For there is still the question which underlies what is called 'the autonomy of ethics'. According to this, the notion that something is right is not logically reducible to any non-ethical notion, such as being commanded by God, or being conducive to happiness, since it is always possible to ask 'But is it always right to do what God commands, or to seek human happiness?' The fact that the question can be asked shows that 'right' cannot just mean what God commands. It may in fact be the case that God always commands what is morally right, but there would have to be reasons additional to the fact of command for believing this to be so, if I am to accept information as to the Will of God as moral information. That the question can significantly be asked shows that what God wills is not *necessarily* coincident with right

To say something is in accordance with the Will of God might be a way of presenting what Matthew Arnold called 'morality tinged with emotion'. It would not then add anything significantly to the meaning of right. On the other hand, if to say something is the Will of God is to say something additional and significant, then the question 'Ought I to do the Will of God?' becomes a genuine one, and the answer might well be 'No', as John Stuart Mill and others have somewhat rhetorically pointed out.

The 'autonomy of ethics' implies that if one is speaking morally, the answer to the moral question cannot be deduced from anything non-moral. One may say, what else would you expect, if one is speaking morally, just as, if one is speaking logically, the demands of logic will be final. But one might be speaking rhetorically, not logically; and one might be speaking religiously, not morally, in a vein in which religious demands are quite different from moral demands. This is a possibility which has not often been taken seriously within the central Jewish-Christian religious tradition, because there has been a built-in connection between morality and the notion of God's commands. Sheer 'theological voluntarism', as it has been called, by which things were right just because God commanded them, has been recessive to the view that God commanded things because they were right, and this was supported by a view that goodness was a necessary attribute of God. Philosophical theologians have struggled over how 'good' can be necessarily predicted of God; and that they have tried to do so at least shows uneasiness about accepting a stark theological voluntarism, with the command-obedience relation as sufficient reason for deciding what one ought to do. This uneasiness can be found even in Hobbes, who comes nearer than most to a strong version of theological voluntarism. Under the rubric 'The Right of God's Sovereignty is derived from his Omnipotence', he says: 'The Right of Nature, whereby God reigneth over men and punisheth those that break his Laws, is to be derived not from his creating them as if he required obedience as of gratitude for his benefits, but from his *Irresistible Power*' (*Leviathan*, Part II, xxxi). Since men are said to break God's Laws and incur punishment 'Omnipotence' and 'Irresistible' are presumably being used not in the sense of the capacity to overwhelm another will, but to command it without allowing recourse to appeal, and with penalties for disobedience which cannot be evaded. For Hobbes, a 'right of nature' is defined in the case of men as the liberty each has to use his power as he will himself for the preservation of his own nature. Since in the case of God this is presumably not in jeopardy, the 'right of nature' would seem simply to be the exercise of his power, without further justification. No doubt by tradition, indeed from his own version of Natural Law, Hobbes also believed in God's goodness; but in relation to men this is subordinate to sheer power to command, which, unlike a sovereignty conferred by pact, rests on no further justification. Hobbes well saw that it was necessary for there to be an unambiguous signalling system by which commands were conveyed. Hence the importance of Moses as lawgiver, and of God's 'Vicegerent', the present Sovereign, as the contemporary authorised interpreter of God's law; 'for when Christian men take not their Christian sovereign for God's prophet, they must either take their own dreams for the Prophecy they mean to be governed by, and the tumour of their own hearts for the spirit of God; or they must suffer themselves to be led by some strange Prince; or by some of their fellow subjects that can bewitch them' (*Leviathan*, Part III, xxxvi).

The interposition of the Sovereign as canalising divine commands is instructive, if repellent. It underlines the inadequacy of the stark notion of command-obedience, by introducing, even within a command model, a notion of legitimate authority in commanding, beyond the notion of mere naked power. This is even more apparent when the authority with right to interpret divine commands is seen as an authoritarian church. The validating claims of the authority need to be accepted for the command to be seen as binding, and if these claims can be questioned in reason and conscience, the moral force of the command can be questioned with them. Indeed, even where the legitimacy of the authority is accepted in general, the moral force of particular commands can be queried, if we admit an element of human judgement as entering into their interpretation, and even notions of 'infallibility' admit this except under strictly qualified conditions. Nevertheless, short of a notion of infallible authority, obedience to commands might be looked on as a way of 'doing the will of God' within a context accepted in conscience, and allowing for the fallibility of the intermediary who does the actual commanding. An instance would be obedience to superiors within a religious community, where the superior is seen as *in loco Dei*, in the sense that a monk may hold that it is the will of God that he should obey his superiors under 'holy obedience', which need not mean that he will not sometimes think their judgement misguided. But in some religious communities, at any rate, superiors are not supposed to exact obedience against a man's conscience; and in all of them it is possible in the last resort to leave the community if the strain on conscience becomes too great. A secular analogy would be the soldier acting under orders. He may only be able to express his feelings about some of them in expletives, but obedience is normally held to be a duty, and not only prudential, because the system within which it is exacted has been accepted. This might need to be qualified in the case of the conscript where there is no allowance for conscientious objection: here obedience might be only prudential and not a moral obligation, and in any case there are times where a plea of obedience to superior orders is not considered to be morally exculpating. Thus, even when obedience is exacted within a context of accepted authority, there is still a place for moral judgement on the part of the individual to whom orders are given. There are two questions here: (*a*) whether the intermediate authority is an authenticated agent, and (*b*) whether it has a *moral* claim to obedience. These tend to be conflated, because there is a general presumption that the orders are given for a good reason. But that these questions can be raised shows that the sheer notion of power to command is not accepted by itself as a moral reason.

Moreover, it is necessary to know what is commanded. If questions can be raised as to whether laws of an authoritarian church are divine commands, so also can they be raised where a person believes he has received a specific *ad hoc* command. Hobbes remarks somewhat cynically that such a one 'being a man, may err, and (which is more) may lie'; and Cromwell exclaimed more sympathetically, 'Truly we have heard many speaking to us and I cannot but think that in many of those things God hath spoke to us . . . and yet there hath been several contradictions in what hath been spoken. But certainly God is not the author of contradictions.'[2] Not only is there the question of the authenticity of the command. Commands should not be ambiguous and problematic, or they are signs of an incompetent and confused authority. Commands can of course, be obeyed simply from fear or prudence, but this is not of interest for the purpose of this discussion. To be of interest, there must be a justification for obedience which is either covertly if not explicitly moral, or which claims there is another demand other than, and higher than, the moral one.

It looks, then, as though the sheer notion of an ultimate religious demand to obey God because of His power to command was seldom the whole story. Even Germans, who have talked, as Germans do (or did), of 'blind obedience' as a virtue, have introduced some vestigially moral notion of a right to command, beyond the stark fact of power. It sometimes sounded as though the Lutheran resisters to the Nazis were confronting an earthly Hitler with a celestial one. But they were also presupposing a long moral tradition, built into Christianity, which made it unlikely, to say the least, that the morally repellent actions of the Nazis could be in accordance with what God commanded. Thus there was still a moral element present in the assertion that one should obey God rather than men. So too was there in fact in Luther. His *'Pecca fortiter'* did not mean that one could commit any crime so long as one was bloody, bold, and resolute, and trusted in God, but that one must live courageously, knowing one is a sinner, and not be obsessed by guilt feelings. Luther was struggling with dark notions of the bondage of the will—*servum arbitrium*—and looking to the liberating power of grace.

Yet the notion of the Grace of God as overcoming the human will, independently of the person's moral judgement, would certainly seem to take us beyond morality. There are views of 'irresistible grace' which clearly take away moral responsibility; others where grace, short of being 'irresistible', is an enabling power by which we can do right actions. Professor Maclagan in *The Theological Frontier of Ethics* (London, 1961) has examined a number of views of this kind from the point of view of one convinced that morality must appeal not only to 'right for right's sake', but to the autonomous, responsible will of the individual, so that in the end

he should be able to say 'it was my own act'. Morality to Maclagan depends, as it does to Kant, on the possibility of a responsible act of our own will. Any view of grace as 'constitutive' of the
will (i.e. making an action not purely our own action) must be
ruled out as destructive of morality. There may be 'environmen-
tal' grace, an influence helping us to do what is right, just as we
may be helped through the encouragement of other people, but
the final decision must be a pure act of the individual's own will.
True, Maclagan says we can never be sure in practice that we
have got this, any more than Kant thought we could be sure in
practice that we were acting from pure good will; but to him, as to
Kant, the notion of the act of pure will is necessary on logical
grounds to secure moral responsibility. This, however, then,
becomes a logical postulate rather than a piece of moral
phenomenology. If we are thinking in terms of the latter, in
practice we can never be sure just where our own free personal
action begins and other people's support or pressure, encouragement or discouragement, ends, so that at some point that one is
able to put one's hand on one's heart and say 'It was all my own
act'. Certainly one must take responsibility, in the sense of being
prepared to be answerable and accountable; and one may give a
final emphasis in acceptance or rejection of the encouragement
and discouragement given by other people. But can one say how
much is due to these and how much to one's own effort?

We are here coming to questions, indeed finally to be faced, of
the sources and supports of morality, which are matters of the
metaphysics or morals. At this stage I am concerned with whether
the religious judgement of what a person ought to do accords with
moral judgement; and if not, which has the last word. If we are
speaking morally, of course the moral judgement has finality. But
suppose we can move into a religious dimension where we are not
speaking morally; where what matters is a relation to God which
is not a matter of morality

Kierkegaard agonised over this in a number of books, especially
in *Fear and Trembling*, where he asks how Abraham could be
justified in being prepared to sacrifice Isaac, an action which
would have been ethically monstrous. Kierkegaard calls this a
'teleological suspension of the ethical'; and by this he means not
that there is a goal for which ethics is suspended, but that there is a
relation of the individual before God which gives rise to a demand
which he thinks is not the same as the ethical demand and is in
potential conflict with it. Ethics, Kierkegaard says, is concerned

with 'the universal'; and he seems to mean by 'the universal' what recent moralists have called 'universalisability'. If it would be right for one to do x in situation S, then it would be right for anyone else similarly placed. 'What is sauce for the goose is sauce for the gander.' This is to say that if there is a rule or reason for doing x, it would not only apply to me individually. The introduction of proper names is not allowed. I cannot say that doing x would be uniquely right for me, Dorothy Emmet, but for no one else. But Kierkegaard is saying that 'The Individual' stands in his uniqueness before God, and may be called on to do something which no one else should do, and for which no rule or reason applicable to anyone else can be given. This is not the amoralism of someone who fails to take ethics seriously. On the contrary; Kierkegaard agonises over the story of Abraham because he sees its horror from an ethical point of view. He contrasts this story with that of Agamemnon sacrificing Iphigenia. This, he says, remains within 'the ethical', because Agamemnon believes that the prospering of his expedition depends on the sacrifice, and his duty as leader of the fleet must come before his love of his daughter. He is obeying a rule that leaders in war must put considerations of success for their expeditions before personal and family considerations, and is doing this in a culture where there was no rule prohibiting human sacrifice.[3] Unlike Agamemnon, Abraham is called to sacrifice Isaac not because of any such principle, and Kierkegaard says the story shows that in faith the individual is above 'the universal'. This presumably means Abraham cannot cite *any* justificatory reason for his action. Faith consists in being the lone individual before God, and this is not the same as being resigned to duty or fate, as Agamemnon could have been and as could also the tragic heroes who suffered for some moral conviction.

Then why did Abraham believe that he was called to sacrifice Isaac? Was it that he needed to do the most costly thing he could in order to prove his love for God? This would give a reason, and is therefore rejected. Was it because he thought he ought to obey what God commanded? The story in Genesis says so, but this would have kept his action still within the sphere of reasons, following a rule that he ought to do what God commanded. Moreover, Kierkegaard is sufficiently sophisticated to see that, whereas in the Genesis story God is represented as actually speaking to Abraham, there can always be a doubt about whether he really did so. So Abraham is not allowed to quote any justificatory reasons which could be put as general rules. This is what, for Kierkegaard, puts him outside the ethical—this, rather than the fact that the proposed act was an ethically monstrous one. But if there was not (as in the original Genesis story) a voice from heaven commanding him, then why should he think that he should sacrifice Isaac?

It might be said that Kierkegaard takes this example just because of its ethical horror. We have seen he also rejects the reasons that this act could be a ritual requirement, or that Abraham ought to give God the most costly thing he could. How costly was pointed out by the Jewish writer, Franz Rosenzweig, in a letter which forms one of a remarkable series written to his friend, the Christian Jew Eugen Rosenstock, in 1916, when they were both in the German army at the front in the First World War:

> You have confused Abraham and Agamemnon. The latter indeed sacrificed what he had for the sake of something else that he wanted, or, if you like, that he considered it his duty to want. . . . But Abraham did not offer something, not 'a' child, but his only son, and what is more, the son of the promise, and sacrificed him to the God of this promise (the traditional Jewish commentary reads this paradox into the text); the meaning of the promise according to human understanding becomes impossible through this sacrifice. Not for nothing is this story associated with our highest festivals; it is the prototype of the sacrifice not of one's person (Golgotha), but of one's existence in one's people, of the 'son' and of all future sons. . . . The son is given back; he is now only the son of the promise. Nothing else happens, no Ilium falls; only the promise remains firm; the father was ready to sacrifice not for the sake of some Ilium, but for the sake of nothing.[4]

Here the 'suspension of the ethical' is even more radical: Abraham is prepared to do something which would put God in the position of breaking his own promise.

It suggests an 'expressive' and not an 'instrumental' act. Abraham was not trying to achieve anything, not even trying to give God a costly present, nor, in Kierkegaard's version, obeying a command. He was showing that his relation to God had an absolute priority. There are indications that Kierkegaard had an autobiographical interest in choosing this story. He had jilted his fiancée, Regine Olsen, not because he did not love her or did not want to marry her, but because he evidently thought his relation to her would get in the way of his absolute relation to God. Regine, he thought, would not have understood this; she was a person who 'would be saved by the finite, not by the infinite'. So he behaved in a way that laid him open to every kind of moral censure.

Kierkegaard is making 'the will of God' a non-moral notion, in which morality is superseded by another kind of demand. This is because he thinks morality needs universalisable rules and reasons, whereas the individual in faith makes a unique decision without these as guides. What then does he go by? Kierkegaard's answer seems to be that he makes an act of pure will. There is a Kantian echo here; but for Kant the pure will is the Good Will which wills a universal law. Here we have the will in stark freedom, either simply in its own right, or as responsible to a hidden God. It is a dizzy prospect; one may well want to say 'Me this uncharted freedom tires'.

It may not only tire; it may produce *Angst*. *Angst* is not fear of anything in particular, but the underlying anxiety produced by the situation of uncertainty and insecurity in which individuals live.

Kierkegaard is looked on as the father of Existentialism, a just ascription in so far as Existentialism is a view which centres on the existing individual as a unique person called to make unique decisions for which no justification can be given in general principles. But Kierkegaard's conclusion on the implication of this for the ultimacy of moral demands is very different from that of the secular Existentialists. Kierkegaard takes the Kantian view of morality as guided by universal principles, and since he holds that the individual no longer has this guidance in decisions made in faith 'before God', then the religious demand goes beyond 'the ethical'. The secular Existentialists, on the other hand, fasten on individual decisions made in freedom without recourse to justification by principles as the only authentic morality. I shall be looking at this claim in the next chapter.

Kierkegaard makes individual decisions in faith before God into ways of expressing the priority given to this relationship, without regard to purpose or principle. 'The Will of God' then becomes an amoral notion, not because it is held to be a source of commands which can go counter to what is morally right, but because the act acknowledging it may do so. The issue for morality then becomes whether in making decisions where there is a reference to the Will of God, an individual should use such moral insights as he can muster in deciding what he should do. By taking faith outside ethics, Kierkegaard is cutting the painter with conscience. In some religious traditions (notably in Protestant Christianity) conscience has been thought of as the link *par excellence* between religion and morality, indeed as 'the voice of God'. In other views it has been seen as the voice of one's old nurse, or the super-ego deposit of authority in childhood. In any case it has been connected with beliefs as to what morally one ought to do.[5] A view which puts doing the Will of God outside conscience is probably as near as we can get to a religious view beyond good and evil. It may be put by appealing to a notion of command without moral authority to command. Or, more subtly, as with Kierkegaard, the call to do the action which goes contrary to morality may be seen as the call to make a gesture expressing the absolute priority given to the relation to God. In either case the priority of conscience is repudiated. If neither of these positions is acceptable in the name of conscience, morality is given the last word. Then, whether the notion of doing the Will of God adds anything to that of doing what is morally right must turn on whether there is a difference between a religiously and a non-religiously motivated conscience. If the notion of conscience is repudiated, then a religious demand which is contrary to it can be given the last word. It would be seen as a demand that made one reject principles, and also presumably final reasons in terms of purposes, except in so far as the intention to give priority to God could be seen as a B-type purpose. It would also be to reject the guidance of one's basic approvals and disapprovals. This is probably as near as we can get to a notion of religion beyond good and evil. It is a possible notion, and if morality is taken completely seriously, then either such a religion must be repudiated, or one would be faced with two conflicting ultimate demands. I shall return to this later. Here I shall follow up the notion of the call to make free decisions where there are no general guiding lights by looking at the secular Existentialists, who see this not as taking one beyond morality, but as the only authentic morality.

9 Existentialist Choice

Existentialism is a theme with many variations. Common to them is the notion of the existing individual as prior to 'essence', a term used generally to stand for any universal 'natures', ends or principles which define a proper pattern for individual conduct. Kierkegaard gave a religious form to the notion of the individual as called to make his own precarious decisions for which no general reasons can be given, and which are made in faith 'before God'. Another founding father of Existentialism, in its secular form, was Nietzsche. Nietzsche does not appear to have known of Kierkegaard, who, after all, wrote in Danish and was not discovered by speakers of main European languages for half a century. Kierkegaard was trying to say what it was like to be the individual 'before God'; Nietzsche, what were the consequences for human action if 'God is dead'. From the extremes of faith and atheism, each reached a position where morality as he defined it was left behind. Kierkegaard, we have seen, defined it in terms of universal principles which cannot provide final guidance to the individual in his lonely decisions. Nietzsche saw 'morality' as the current blend of Christianity and Utilitarianism which he thought had together put across the notion that the few strong and creative characters should serve the many weak and pusillanimous ones. The man who sees this must be prepared to be 'beyond Good and Evil', Nietzsche's own phrase but one which is ambiguous, especially in Nietzsche himself.

Nietzsche says different things at different times. Much of his writing is aphoristic, a style which lends itself to impressionistic utterance rather than argument. Sometimes when he speaks of 'good and evil', he is seeing these in terms of the social morality he despises. At the same time, in putting forward a 'transvaluation of values', he is redefining good and evil in the terms of an alternative morality of a highly elitist kind. This alternative morality will be one in which 'The great epochs of our lives are the points when we gain courage to rebaptize our badness as the best in us'

(*Beyond Good and Evil*, §116). But if 'badness' is rebaptised, could it not be given the name of 'goodness'?

When Nietzsche speaks like this of 'beyond good and evil', he is in fact using a rhetorical device while advocating an alternative morality to replace that which he despises. He is giving what one might call an 'anti-persuasive definition'. But he also uses the phrase 'beyond good and evil' to make a more philosophical point. It is that good and evil have no existence outside the human will, which creates its own morality. This is to repudiate any grounding of good and evil in transcendental or supernatural reality; the man who is 'beyond good and evil' has shed this illusion (which can yet be fostered through art). Such a man 'creates a goal for mankind and gives the earth its meaning and its future: he it is who *creates* the quality of good and evil in things'.[1] If good and evil have no reality outside the human will, popularly this can be taken as moral nihilism, and Nietzsche's rhetoric can suggest this. Logically, it is the view that values are created by human choice, and the choice can be made seriously. For Nietzsche, it is of qualities which enhance power, courage, heroic virtue (in the Renaissance sense of *virtù*). So 'the Will to Power' both stands for a meta-ethical view that values are subjectively created, and also suggests substantive values of a particular kind.

So the final call is to the supreme effort this demands, and it is the creative, superior person who will make it. Most people try to cushion themselves against the effort by the self-protective devices of social morality. Social morality, especially under Christian influence, is a 'herd morality', a 'slave morality'. There are places where Nietzsche puts his finger on the self-deceptions in this kind of morality. The ideal of humility can mask the fact that it is easier to be a small man—one is less vulnerable, and the risks of failure are less. Zarathustra's 'last men' huddle together and are comfortable, and make everything small. They rub up together because they need warmth, and do not go where it is hard to live (*Thus Spake Zarathustra, Vorrede* 5). And again: 'What is "virtue" and "charity" in Christianity if not just this mutual preservation, this solidarity of the weak, this hampering of selection? What is Christian altruism if not the mass-egoism of the weak, which divines that if all care for one another each individual will be preserved as long as possible?' (*The Will to Power*, II, §246). To live so as to achieve, not just so as to exist, means 'one must be cruel and inexorable towards all that becomes old and weak in ourselves, and not only in ourselves' (*The Gay Science*, ૪ 26).

Nietzsche's view is meta-ethically one of an autonomy of moral-ity in which man creates his own good and evil in a world in which 'God is dead'. The creation of morality is an expression of 'the Will to Power'. But the meta-ethical and the substantive levels are not so independent that Nietzsche's view of autonomy could be consonant with *any* substantive morality. This is due, at least in part, to the ambiguity in the notion of 'the Will to Power'. This can mean recognising that one is autonomous, but since this takes courage, it will be the superior type of person who will rise to it. Thus we have not a two-tier view of meta-ethics and substantive ethics, but rather an ethical theory the logic of which favours a particular style of life. 'The Will to Power' is indeed the will to create one's own values, but it is also a will which has the qualities which Nietzsche thinks are needed to undertake this. So the notion of 'will' is not purely formal, and its 'freedom' is given a content in terms of power over oneself as well as over others. 'Power' here is not crude domination, though latter-day degener-ate Germans who fed on Nietzsche's headier passages may have seen it like that. It is the quality needed for the self-affirmation of the creative person who can pay the cost of this affirmation.

'That which is termed "freedom of the will" is essentially the emotion of supremacy in respect to him who must obey' (*Beyond Good and Evil*, §19). The one who must obey may be another part of oneself, or it may be another person. In one's own case, where the will is a self-mastery, 'the person exercising volition adds the feelings of delight of his successful executive instruments, the useful "under-wills" or under-souls—indeed, our body is but a social structure composed of many souls—to his feelings of delight as commander...'. The effectiveness of will is a way of acting in which organic function, impulse, passion, thought, can be inte-grated, and this is 'the Will to Power'. It is to be asserted, not denied; and in asserting it, tendencies generally labelled bad—aggressive and violent tendencies, subtle and dissembling powers—can also contribute, and they must be integrated and used.

As an advocate of the will which creates its own values, Nietzsche is a forerunner of Existentialism. The characteristic Existentialist notion, however, is not 'the Will to Power', but freedom of choice. In choice we are aware of alternative pos-sibilities of action; the Existentialist would say that freedom con-sists not only in this but in assuming responsibility for whatever alternative we take. This is not a particular mental act of volition, an act of 'setting oneself to do' (a well-known phrase of H. A. Prichard's). It is the person acting as chooser, and taking responsibility for choosing. Existentialists would therefore probably endorse Locke's saying that 'we do better to speak of the man as free than of the will as free'.

> We find in ourselves a power to begin or forbear, continue or end several actions of our minds, and motions of our bodies. This power which the mind has thus to order the consideration of any idea, or the forbearing to consider it; or to prefer the motion of any part of the body to its rest . . . is that which we call the *Will*. The actual exercise of that power, by directing any particular action, or its forbearance is that which we call *volition* or *willing*. . . . So far as a man has power to think or not to think, to move or not to move, according to the preference or direction of his own mind, so far is a man *free*.

And since to speak of the will as the commanding and superior faculty of the soul suggests a confused notion of faculties as so many distinct agents in us, we do better to speak of the *man* as free than of the *will* as free. If then a man is said to 'will', he must have preferences, i.e. be able to make comparisons between alternatives and choose between them (*An Essay concerning Human Understanding* II, xxi, §§ 5, 8, 21).

For Existentialists the human being is always in a position where he has a choice between alternative possibilities; even where he is continuing on a set course, he is choosing to do this rather than (in Locke's term) to forbear. This is his freedom; and the acceptance and exercise of this freedom does not take the Existentialist beyond morality; it is the only authentic morality. This may look like a meta-ethical view of what it is to be moral, but, as with other meta-ethics, it is not neutral; it has normative consequences in how people think they should behave, and we shall be noting some of them.

To say that man has freedom of choice is here to say that he creates his values through his choices. He does not choose values as established features or properties of anything in the world, either metaphysically or sociologically. Even if they so appear, it is always open to him to question their value. (One recalls Moore's open-ended question to any naturalistically proffered value: 'Is it good?', though of course, the Existentialist would not subscribe to the view that anything could have an intuitable non-natural property of goodness.) But Existentialists have one non-optional value, that of freedom to choose, and their substantive morality can take the form of a preoccupation with its exercise. If one appraises free choice just because it is free choice, then, though what in fact one chooses need not be immaterial, it may become so, and what matters is that one chooses. So Kirillov in Dostoevsky's *The Possessed* talks about committing suicide just to show that he is free to do so. However, one suspects that he fastens on suicide not just because this would be an example of a free act, but because it would be such an outrageous example; also that he wants to show that 'if God is dead, then everything is permitted', so that it is an act of emancipation.

The emphasis on the value of choosing as such is sometimes put in difficult language about 'choosing oneself', or of the will willing itself. If the will is simply willing itself, without willing to achieve or express anything else, some content must be given to the notion of 'choice of oneself'; if it is a demand for self-knowledge, it could be finding out what sort of person I am, what I really want, and giving this as my reason for choosing to do x rather than y. I do x because I really want to—not because it would be the correct, approved, prudent thing to do. It may be any one or all of these, and yet I may choose not to do it.

This can be an exercise in self-knowledge, in trying to find what I myself really think and what I really want. But to know whether I really choose x, I need to get as clear a perception as possible of what x is like. The Existentialist is thus concerned with two things: what x is like and his freedom in choosing x, and he can become absorbed in the latter.

This may be why people influenced by Existentialist views are preoccupied with trying to discover their 'identity', 'who they are', what they really want; their values are sincerity and single-mindedness in acting accordingly. This may be the morality of one particular life-style—giving absolute priority to the process of 'becoming oneself', and since one is preoccupied with looking at oneself, I call it moral Narcissism.

The notion of one's 'identity' as something to be found was, I think, popularised from Eric Erikson's *Childhood and Society* (1950). Erikson has reviewed and revised his earlier views in a book called *Identity: Youth and Crisis*. He uses 'identity' to mean the secure sense of being a person in relation to other persons, with one's own beliefs and convictions. This is not described as a task of an isolated individual, but a process, largely unconscious, in which first a child, then an adolescent, and finally a grown person develops from the stage of 'identification with' various figures towards having his own standards.[2]

There can be a 'crisis of identity', where an individual cannot establish how he sees himself in relation to others. This also has become a vogue expression. Erikson mentions a notice in which the Catholic students of Harvard announced that they would be holding an Identity Crisis on Thursday night at eight o'clock sharp.

Erikson's use is by no means moral Narcissism; it describes growth into being an independent person in relation to others. The Existentialist preoccupation with 'identity' cuts off from other factors the concern consciously to assert one's own freedom. If, on the other hand, a person grows and develops through learning to appreciate things, this will mean that he is interested in them and not only in his own identity. The parochial nature of this interest in one's own identity has been characterised by Lévi-Strauss, who calls Existentialism

> cette entreprise auto-admirative où, non sans jobardise, l'homme contemporain s'enferme en tête-à-tête avec lui-même et tombe en extase devant soi—se coupe d'un savoir scientifique qu'on méprise et d'une humanité réelle dont on méconnait la profondeur historique et les dimensions ethnographiques, pour se ménager un petit monde clos et réservé: Café du Commerce idéologique où, pris entre les quatre murs d'une condition humaine taillée à la mesure d'une société particulière, des habitués ressassent à longueur de journée des problèmes d'intérêt local, au delà desquels l'atmosphère enfumée de leur tabagie dialectique les empêche de porter la vue.[3]
>
> . . . an exercise in self-admiration in which contemporary man is duped, shut up in colloquy with himself, prostrate in ecstasy before himself. It is cut off from scientific knowledge which is despised, and genuine humanity whose historical depth and ethnographical dimensions are not recognised, in order to set up a closed and private world; an ideological saloon bar where the habitués, safely inside the four walls of a human condition made to the measure of a specific society,

all day long go over problems of local interest, beyond which the smoky atmosphere of their dialectical fug prevents them from seeing.

Such a narrow horizon may indeed be characteristic of popular Existentialism in the cafés. It would, however, not be fair to the more serious Existentialists, notably Sartre; who are indeed aware of important and difficult moral problems. These arise in particular situations, under conditions of uncertainty, and where it is unlikely that any action that is taken will be unequivocally satisfactory. Nevertheless, for Sartre, in making decisions, my 'project' is to become a certain kind of person. I am not determined by my character, because at each stage I am making it by my choices. In these I am acting in a way which expresses the person I myself am choosing to be. I am not just choosing to be the kind of person whom I could admire in what sociologists would call my 'reference group'—or, if I am, it must be because I myself choose to be like this, in my own way, which will be subtly different from anyone else's way.

The emphasis on free choice distinguishes this from an 'emotive' view, where ethical utterances, whether about my own or other people's actions, are said to express feelings. In choosing I am not expressing my feelings; I am making a decision, and am making it through choosing to be a certain kind of person. Perhaps 'kind of person' suggests too much generality. If not even this much concession can be made to generality, then it is very difficult to see how I can be thinking at all about what I should do. Without thinking, I could just react, or simply assert myself. But is to react or assert oneself the same as to choose? If I am to choose, I must have more than one possibility before me, and also some means of distinguishing between the possibilities. The Existentialist may say this can be granted, but that in the end which possibility I choose will depend on an emphasis I give to my own inner awareness of myself as someone I am coming to be.

This is 'authentic' action, as distinct from action in 'bad faith'. Authentic action might be described as the choice of one's own life-style. 'Bad faith' is the evasion of responsibility for choice by acting in ways which are really governed by conformity with a social role or by other people's expectations and opinions, without owning to myself that this is what I am doing; if I *choose* to play the role, and to play it in my own way, that need not be bad faith.

Existentialists are prepared to call this choice of a life style *ethics*. Mary Warnock, in discussing Sartre,[4] denies them this right, since 'ethics must be defined as the theory of how people should live *together*' (her italics). I am inclined also to italicise '*must be*'. Mary Warnock is giving a stipulative definition of ethics, which is truncated because it fastens on the social aspect and omits the aspect of commitment to a chosen life-style, guided by one's basic approvals. If one fastens on the latter aspect, then an Existentialist view could be an ethical view, and what is at stake is how satisfactory it is, since it also is a truncated one.

For the Existentialist, the authentic way of life is single-minded commitment to one's freedom; whatever the decision, it should be *my* decision for which I take responsibility. There is a Kantian echo here, but the notion of the will is that of sheer freedom of choice, not of the pure will as the rational good will guided by respect for the moral law. The Existentialist takes the Kantian notion of the free will as self-legislating to an extreme where the will has only itself to go by. The moral question is not 'What ought I to do?', but 'What do I myself decide to do?' If the point is not to decide what I ought to do, but that I ought to do whatever I decide to do, the moral weight rests on the notion of sheer decision as such.

Any view of the autonomy of ethics has to put the weight on decision as distinct from factual knowledge. But if this is not to be arbitrary, the notion of decision will need to be supplemented by some recommendation about what we want ethics for. Kant indeed thought that the rational will could provide its own content by willing a categorical imperative which it would be inconsistent to reject. You could not will that everyone should tell lies, because then no one would believe you, and so universal lying would be self-defeating. But this test has only limited applications. Others will find a content for morality by saying that we can decide what would be the conditions for the kind of community in which we would choose to live. Such a view might combine the notion of choice with some form of social contract theory. But any contract view involves my accepting limitations on my future freedom of choice, on certain conditions also accepted by other people. This would not be congenial to Existentialists, who want to leave freedom of choice between possibilities open at every stage. They may not go so far as the Leveller Buff-coat, who said to Cromwell, in his own theological language, 'That whatsoever hopes or obligations I should be bound unto, if afterward God should reveal himself, I would break it speedily, if it were an hundred a day.'[5] But by insisting that authentic action depends on open-ended choice, they make it difficult to do justice to the extent to which social morality depends on shared expectations as to how, generally speaking, one can count on people behaving.[6]

This is not to say that Existentialists reject the notion of commitment, though there may well be a problem in finding a cause to which one can be wholeheartedly committed—'*engagé*'. Sartre, who has always been a politically involved Existentialist, speaks in his latest writings of the possibility of belonging to a group to which one is pledged. Such a group is seen in Marxist terms as claiming an absolute commitment of its members, in conflict with other groups in a liberation struggle. This notion of a fused group offers commitment to a joint project, but is an incomplete answer to the question of how to see mutual obligations within a social morality. The individual, creating his own life against the threats to his freedom constituted by other people, is replaced by the group in conflict with other groups. In *L'Être et le Néant* (*Being and Nothingness*, E. T. London, 1957) Sartre developed a view of how we may be said to eat up each other's freedom. A person can only exist in relation to other people. But they see him through his body as an object, while he sees himself subjectively as his own project of the self he is seeking to become. These two views could only completely coincide if a person could either make himself into a doormat-like object for other people (Masochism), or use them as objects for his own free project (Sadism). Or he might try and make himself indifferent to how they see him. None of these possibilities is in fact successful.

Sartre is emphasising that there is always a certain opaqueness in people's mutual knowledge of each other, and this makes for tragedy; he is stressing failure in communication rather than perceptiveness as inherent in these relations; indeed, he is taking a view of the autonomy of the self as a being freely creating his own good and evil which could only be successful if there were only one such. The model would be the God of voluntarist theology, depending on nothing but the fiat of his own will. And since the human condition does not admit of this absolute independence (what the theologians called *aseitas*), 'man is a useless passion' (*Being and Nothingness*, English translation, p. 615).

It is possible to move from the tragic view, where frustration is inherent in the human situation, to a view which fastens on contingency as in itself a perverse kind of value. This comes out in the notion of the *acte gratuit*. Life is absurd, and there need be no reason or purpose in what I do beyond the fact that I choose to do it. Some Existentialists, such as Gide, and Camus in *The Myth of Sisyphus*, write like this, but it is not the most serious strain in Existentialist ethics, and was indeed repudiated by Sartre. It is, however, literally the *reductio ad absurdum* of a view which makes freedom of choice not only the source of values, but the one absolute value.

If the Existentialists were only saying that I often have to act in problematic situations where I have to choose between alternatives under uncertainty, and that I must take responsibility for my choice, they would be saying something no doubt true, but not very original. So too, when they present whatever we choose as likely to be far from satisfactory—that we are continually faced with what we call a choice of evils is also, I believe, true, and less often allowed for by moralists. The Existentialists go to the limit in pressing the autonomy of ethics, not as a meta-ethical view, but as the style of life of a moral subject, whose reasons for action can only be good reasons because he himself chooses to make them so. This must surely make it hard to see how he can *think* what he should do, except as an inward-looking exercise in discovering what fits his own chosen life-style. Existentialists say what is good is made so by my choice, but they also use 'good' of the act of choosing itself. This makes goodness internal to willing without Kant's constraints on the good will as rationally willing the moral law. They may reasonably query the notion of a moral *law*, but in its place they leave us with a will which wills itself. If this is not to be an empty notion, it has to be taken as a person's choice and affirmation of his own life-style. He therefore needs to be able to find a life-style which he does not feel to be bogus, or imposed on him by convention. We have here a B-type teleology, of seeking and affirming a certain orientation in whatever one does. Since I have said that I think that a B-type teleology is the most defensible kind of moral stance, it might be thought that I should have been more sympathetic than I have been to the Existentialists. I go with them in thinking that moral judgements must be made in the first person, that they involve risks, and that one must take responsibility for them. But I would not say that because reasons for action may not be demonstratively compelling, they may not nevertheless be what Mill calls 'considerations capable of determining the intellect', and I shall later try

and look at some of these. Nor would I go with the Existentialists when they turn the assertion that one should take
responsibility for choice into a notion that this is somehow
choosing oneself. Also, though their view of morality may not be
simple to live by, it is nevertheless over-simple in how it sees
social morality.

The Existentialists are right, I think in connecting their moral
view with a moral psychology. They see the human being as continually choosing, called on to realise this overtly and to take
responsibility for his choices. I have tried to pinpoint the limit-
ation I see in this moral psychology[7] by calling it 'Moral
Narcissism', in so far as it concentrates attention on making one's
own choice as distinct from an interest in what one thinks worth
choosing and why. In the B-type orientation which I would
advocate (I shall try to say more about this in Chapter 12) I
would want to displace the Existentialist notion of choice of oneself by a notion of 'liberty of spirit'. To seek liberty of spirit
is to try to get rid of the fears, self-deceptions, prejudices which
hinder one from getting a clear view of the situations in which
one must act, and trying to estimate what one should do in them.
Liberty of spirit is not just 'liberation' for its own sake, but a
condition in which I can best carry out whatever purposes I
believe to be worth pursuing and in which I may be able to see
more clearly the impact on other people of what I am doing.
Attending to it is therefore singling out a band in the moral
spectrum in a way which also lights up other colours, such as
purpose, principle and appraisal, whereas Existentialists are
seeing one band—that of the call for personal and responsible
choice. Other bands—notably principle and purpose—are seen
as only taking colour from that of choice. Principles then become
my own self-legislation in a far more radical sense than Kant's.[8]
What about purpose? Existentialists speak of my project in
creating myself as what I choose to be. But this collapses into the
notion of choice as guided by preoccupation with my 'identity'.
This view of purpose would be less inward-looking if it were the
single-minded pursuit of some form of achievement which I
choose, as what is popularly called 'doing my thing', or in more
solemn language as finding my vocation.

I shall now turn to looking at the adequacy of such single-
mindedness to provide an ethical way of life; is such single-
mindedness unqualifiedly a virtue?

10 Single-mindedness

Kierkegaard can again give us a point of departure. In a series of meditations called *Purify your Hearts: Spiritual Preparation for the Office of Confession*[1] he says that 'purity of heart is to will one thing', and that what is so willed is 'the Good'. We have seen that Kierkegaard's man of faith makes free decisions which are said to take him beyond 'the ethical'. Here he is apparently saying that if one is sufficiently single-minded so as to will one thing, that will be 'the Good'. This has an almost Platonic ring about it. I do not want to embark on exegesis of Kierkegaard, but to note that he has called good what one whole-heartedly wills. Elsewhere he says it is 'to choose oneself in freedom'.[2] Is 'the Good' whatever it may be that one whole-heartedly wills? Or could one only whole-heartedly (or pure-heartedly, if that is the same thing) will what is good?

There is indeed, a sense in which if anyone is whole-heartedly set on something, this may be called his good. Milton's Satan could say, 'Evil, be thou my good'; he calls evil not 'good', but 'my good'. One may start from the sheer fact of desiring something and say with Hobbes that 'good and evil signify only our appetites and aversions'. But few are content to leave it at that, since we appeal to others to share our approvals. C. L. Stevenson's well-known analysis of '*x* is good' into 'I approve of *x*: do so too',[3] though overtly a statement of fact coupled with a command, is more like an appeal. Why, after all, should you share my approval just because I tell you to? I am commending rather than commanding.

If I am commending, my approval should be steady, not erratic. I can look at something steadily without letting my other concerns distract me. Or if I do let myself be distracted, in a cool hour I can bring myself back to my verdict, or—since such verdicts need not be beyond appeal—I can quietly reconsider it. The point is that there is undistracted consideration: if I then judge that something is good, I can ask if it is worthy of whole-hearted approval; if I am not prepared to make the judgement whole-heartedly, I then wonder whether it is really good.

I shall be returning to the question of 'the Good' in a later context.[4] What I have said shortly about it here is a preliminary to looking further into Kierkegaard's saying that if one could will one thing, it would be 'the Good'. Again, my concern is not commentary on Kierkegaard, but to take his saying and ask whether whole-heartedness, or single-mindedness, is in itself a condition in which what is willed is good, or could there be a whole-hearted willing of something which was not good, at least in any sense other than that in which one might call anything one makes one's project one's 'good'.

When I have spoken of whole-heartedness, or single-mindedness, Kierkegaard speaks of 'purity of heart'. This may not be the same thing, but if 'purity of heart' is to will one thing, single-mindedness must be at least a necessary, if not a sufficient condition. Desires come and go and are ambivalent. 'Willing one thing' must overcome this ambivalence. Its opposite is double-mindedness. Kierkegaard has a gallery of double-minded people, notably those who are concerned not just for 'the good' but for their own success in achieving it, so that they are willing not one thing but two—the good and their own success. If I want 'the good' single-mindedly, I would rejoice equally if it came about through somebody else.

To will is to seek to bring something about, not only to appreciate it. Single-mindedness in willing one thing suggests giving this absolute priority, even if one is glad for it to be accomplished in the end by others rather than oneself. It therefore raises the question of whether to give any particular end an absolute priority (an A-type teleology) can be a sufficient moral view, even if one accepts the worthiness of the end. If it can, the question 'Ought I to give this priority in these particular circumstances?' is not allowed to arise as a moral question because it has already been settled.

There may indeed be such a single-minded dedication; it is shown particularly in the lives of some artists. In discussing the difference between the moral and the aesthetic attitude to life, I said that the aesthetic was a spectator's attitude carried over into conduct. The person who is totally dedicated to producing what is of aesthetic value is not thereby taking up an aesthetic attitude. He is deciding to give this task absolute priority over any other possible claim, and this, I said, was a problem within morality, and not between morality and something outside it. It is a particular case of vocational dedication, and produces the moral question of conflicts between the claims of dedication to some achievement and of obligations to other people.[5] The lives of artists raise this question in an acute form, perhaps because of the extreme concentration they need for their art, and because, particularly in the case of music and painting, it may be possible for them to separate their thoughts about their work from their thoughts about other people.

There is the stuff of tragedy here, and it is the more acute in that what is achieved at the cost of other people may indeed be something great and splendid. A fictional example is that of Charles Strickland in Somerset Maugham's *The Moon and Sixpence*. Strickland follows an imperious urge to be a painter at desperate cost to himself and to other people, particularly to the women in his life. In the end he dies of leprosy in a South Sea island, having covered the walls of his hut with astounding pictures, and when dying he orders the hut to be burnt down. It may be that wanting to destroy one's work is—fortunately for us—rare in real life, and perhaps the sign of a fanatic. It may even be a sign that 'purity of heart' has not been achieved, since it suggests that the person wants not that the work should be done, but that he should do it, and be able to prove to himself that he can do it. But in any case, the will to do it has become a single imperative passion.

Another fictional example is one to which I have already referred—Dubedat in Shaw's *The Doctor's Dilemma*. That Dubedat is a ham artist rather than a great one does not prevent him from claiming that for the sake of his art he is justified in behaving in ways which could be called morally unscrupulous. When he dies, his wife Jennifer says, 'He sacrificed everything for his art. In a certain sense he had even to sacrifice everybody.' The Doctor, Ridgeon, comments 'Everybody except himself. By keeping that back he lost the right to sacrifice you, and gave me the right to sacrifice him. Which I did.' Then Jennifer says, 'He was one of those men who know what women know: that self-sacrifice is vain and cowardly.' Ridgeon says, 'Yes, when the sacrifice is rejected and thrown away. Not when it becomes the food of godhead.' Jennifer replies 'I do not understand that.'

Bernard Williams in a paper 'Moral Luck' (*Aristotelian Society*, Supplementary Volume L, 1976) takes 'Gauguin' as a stock figure for a person who neglects the claims of his family for his art. Not perhaps altogether fairly. Gauguin was not unconcerned about his wife and children. His wife could not take to an artist's bohemian life, and returned with her younger children to her own people in Copenhagen. Gauguin tried at first to keep his eldest son with him in Paris, but was too poor to provide for him, so the boy went to the in-laws, who seem to have been quite well off. Gauguin continued to correspond with his wife, and when he painted pictures he sent her canvasses to sell. True, he went to Tahiti, and paid his passage out of their joint property without her consent. But we should not overdo the extent to which he dismissed the claims of his wife and children. However, Williams' 'Gauguin' is a type figure, not meant to be cast biographically, and we are concerned with what he typifies. Williams says he is not morally justified at the time of his decision, and at that time he could not know that he would be justified by success. His justification depended on luck, i.e. on factors outside his control. 'Gauguin' was therefore weighing moral considerations about his family against a gamble on the possibility of producing great art, and this could be justified, if it was, only if he did produce it, a justification which he could not have had when he made his decision to go to Tahiti. Unlike Williams, I see this still as a problem within morality. 'Gauguin' has to decide whether to take the risk of going all out for his art at the expense of his wife and family, so the question is that of pursuit of a dominant aim at cost to others as well as himself. The trouble about Dubedat, though not perhaps about the actual Gauguin, was that he lacked self-knowledge of his own powers, and he took the sacrifice of other people for granted, not even seeing that there was a moral problem.

A telling example of the problem from real life is given by Françoise Gilot in her book *Life with Picasso*; it is the more telling in that Picasso himself sees and states it. Picasso is urging Françoise to leave her grandmother, who had given her a home when she ran away from her parents, and to come and live with him.

'Look at it this way,' he said. 'What you can bring to your grandmother, aside from the affection you have for her, is not something essentially constructive. When you're with me, on the other hand, you help me to realize something very constructive. It's more logical and more positive for you to be close to me, in view of the fact that I really need you. As far as your grandmother's feelings are concerned, there are things one can

do and make them understood, and there are other things that
can only be done by *coup d'état* since they go beyond the limits
of another person's understanding. It's almost better to strike
a blow and after people have recovered from it, let them accept
the fact.' I told him that sounded rather brutal to me.

'But there are some things you can't spare other people,' he
said. 'It may cost a terrible price to act in this way but there are
moments in life when we don't have a choice. If there is one
necessity which for you dominates all others, then necessarily
you must act badly in some respect. There is no total, absolute
purity other than the purity of refusal. In the acceptance of a
passion one considers extremely important and in which one
accepts for oneself a share of tragedy, one steps outside the
usual laws and has the right to act as one should not act under
ordinary conditions.' I asked him how he arrived at that
rationalization.

'At a time like that, the sufferings one has inflicted on others,
one begins to inflict on oneself equally,' he said. 'It's a question
of the recognition of one's destiny and not a matter of unkindness or insensitivity. Theoretically one might say one hasn't the
right to reach out for a share of happiness, however minute it
may be, which rests on someone else's misfortune, but the
question can't be resolved on that theoretical basis. We are
always in the midst of a mixture of good and evil, right and
wrong, and the elements of any situation are always hope-
lessly tangled. One person's good is antagonistic to another's.
To choose one person is always, in a measure, to kill someone
else. And so one has to have the courage of the surgeon or the
murderer, if you will, and to accept the share of guilt which
that gives, and to attempt, later on, to be as decent about it as
possible. In certain situations one can't be an angel.'

I told him that a primitive person could face up to that idea
much more easily than someone who thought in terms of principles of good and evil and who tried to act on the basis of
them.

'Never mind your theories,' he said. 'You must realize that
there is a price on everything in life. Anything of great value—
creation, a new idea—carries its shadow zone with it. You have
to accept it that way. Otherwise there is only the stagnation of
inaction. But every action has an implicit share of negativity.
There is no escaping it. Every positive value has its price in

negative terms and you never see anything very great which is
not, at the same time, horrible in some respect. The genius of
Einstein leads to Hiroshima.'[6]

Note that Picasso is defending a philosophy of the cost of doing
creative work, and this includes his being prepared to carry a
burden of guilt in personal relations. In so far as this is a considered decision about a policy for living, it is in that sense a moral
decision. But it was a decision which demanded that other people
besides Picasso himself should be subordinated to his creative
work. Some people are prepared for such subordination, and may
indeed even find their own fulfilment in it. Françoise was prepared to foster the intense self-concentration which Picasso
needed for his work, but his insistence on subordinating her to
his own life did not stop there. She was no doormat, but a strong-
minded woman who was also a painter in her own right. She
came to the point of needing to establish that she also had a life
to live, and she threatened to leave him.

Now it was Pablo's turn to laugh at *me*. 'You imagine
people will be interested in *you?*' he said. 'They won't ever,
really, just for yourself. Even if you think people like you, it will
only be a kind of curiosity they will have about a person whose
life has touched mine so intimately. And you'll be left with only
the taste of ashes in your mouth. For you, reality is finished;
it ends right here. If you attempt to take a step outside my
reality—which has become yours, in as much as I found you
when you were young and unformed and I burned everything
around you—you're headed straight for the desert. And if you
go, that's exactly what I wish for you.'
I told him I had no doubt that the majority of people who
now bent over backward to please me acted that way for
reasons that were neither pure nor sincere. But if I was destined
to live in the desert, as he predicted, I wanted to make the
effort to do just that, and to see if I could survive, if for no
other reason than to find out what I was. For ten years now I
had lived in his shadow, trying wholeheartedly most of the
time to relieve the pain of his solitude. But since I now realized
that he lived in a self-enclosed world and that his solitude was
therefore total, I wanted to explore my own solitude.

'Your job is to remain by my side, to devote yourself to me and to the children', he said. 'Whether it makes you happy or unhappy is no concern of mine. If your presence here provides happiness and stability for others, that's all you should ask.' I told him it was quite clear from his recent performance that I couldn't do much about providing *him* with any stability, and as far as the children were concerned, I was no longer convinced that they would have less stability without him than they had with us together. He grew very angry. . . .

It was apparently pointless to try to make him see anything unrealistic in his notion that one of us should be motivated only by a sense of duty and have no feelings whatever, while the other should react only in accordance with his feelings and have no sense of duty toward anyone but himself. Pablo always saw himself as a river sweeping everything before it. That was his nature and he must obey it. He used to refer to himself as 'an ascetic of the plethora'. His vision of my role was that of the unresisting saint, sitting quietly in her cave, sanctifying or at least neutralizing by an exemplary existence the worst aspects of his own way of life. At one time I had been able to accept that concept. But now the distance between us had grown too great.[7]

So she walked out.

There is danger in these cases that what started as single-minded dedication can end as egoistic self-centredness, the person surrounding himself with those who will give him unquestioning service, instead of with people with minds and wills of their own who can stand up to him and give him criticism he may well need. It is tempting to think that this could in the end have a corrupting effect on his work, and this may indeed have been so in Picasso's case, if we are to believe the picture given in John Berger's *Success and Failure of Picasso* (Penguin, 1965), where there is a picture of the aged artist keeping court with sycophantic admirers, devoted to his own creativity, and running out of subjects to paint. It may be a moralist's wishful thinking to suppose that such selfishness will corrupt the work; it may, however, corrupt the person, if relations with other people are an inescapable part of life, so that in excluding them from one's moral view one may thicken one's sensibilities. Or one may admit and then dismiss the thought, carrying suppressed guilt feelings.

I started this chapter with Kierkegaard's saying that 'Purity of heart is to will one thing', and I have ended with the dilemma of a possible clash between single-minded dedication and the claims of personal relations. Single-mindedness, when it produces a hardening of sensibility to other people, may not be the same as 'purity of heart'. It may strengthen concentration on a single purpose; it may also subtly lead to ambition and love of power. While these may increase determination, they may also come to take precedence over the purpose itself.

> For those who serve the greater cause may make the cause serve them,
> Still doing right,

Thomas à Becket says in Eliot's *Murder in the Cathedral*. 'Purity of heart' calls for clear perception not only of one's central purpose but of one's motives in pursuing it.

There is a narrow borderline between purity of heart and singleness of mind in the pursuit of an end, but it is there, and much religious teaching is concerned with it. The daemonic person has an inner discipline, but he has a close connection between dedication to his end and self-assertion in following it. His inner asceticism may turn him into a fanatic. A daemonic person need not be a fanatic; he may be too intelligent. But his self-assertion may cut him off from sources of criticism, and so too possibilities of co-operation with others. Hitler was an extreme example, and he corrupted others who had fed on Nietzschean ideas of the Superman, and then brutalised them. He may have been an obsessional fanatic from the start; he also had a charismatic quality which could sway—perhaps even hypnotise—others.

The daemonic person has a specific aim (Teleology A), but he also lives in a way in which following it is combined with self-assertion (Teleology B). Single-mindedness need not become daemonic, and there are, of course, diversities of aims, and it may be possible to pursue an unworthy one with a dedication worthy of a better cause. Teleological views of morality have usually looked for criteria in the value of the aim. But the problem goes deeper than this. It is the problem of whether a teleological view which gives absolute priority to any specific aim however high, is an adequate moral view. Such a view fastens on factors of purpose and appraisal of the value of the purpose, claiming the right to subordinate or ignore factors such as civic duties and the personal claims of other people. Those with something really important to do may well become egoists in order to avoid distractions. If they are not egoists they will have to live with tensions which cannot, I believe, be resolved by finding some master principle of morality which can assign priorities in every situation. The tension will be recognised if one allows regard for other people to be an element within the complex of considerations which go into the essentially contestable concept of morality. Since relations with other people are an inescapable part of life, how one thinks one should behave in these relations, if it is only by a decision to ignore them as far as possible, should surely be an ingredient in morality, even if it is not the whole of it. It may well be that the person with a high degree of dedication to what he sees as a supremely important work will make this work the dominant moral factor. The popular picture of Christian ethics which centres it on a cosy view of family relations is hardly borne out by the saying in the Gospels that in order to be Christ's disciple one must be ready to hate father and mother—and yet the command to love one's neighbour is also in the Gospel, presenting if not relieving the tension. This may be why those who believe themselves called to follow some extreme vocation have often been celibate. 'He that hath wife and children', says Bacon, 'hath given hostages to fortune; for they are impediments to great enterprises, either of virtue or mischief.' Yet celibacy is manifestly a non-universalisable principle. If one refines the principle by saying that those set on great enterprises should be celibate, this would surely suggest that the majority of mankind must set their sights too low. One may try to see more clearly the implications of what one is undertaking, both in the enterprise and in one's personal relations, and in both cases be prepared for the unexpected demand. One's view of morality must, I believe, start from this complexity. The person who sees his morality as giving absolute priority to a particular aim may acquire a blinkered view which narrows his vision, and then try to justify this by downgrading social morality.[8]

The contrary simplification is to define morality purely in terms of what I have just called social morality, and to ignore the morality internal to one's effort to achieve whatever it may be (not necessarily only one thing) that one thinks important to achieve. If it be said that few people are dedicated in a single-minded way to great enterprises, and not all that many are worried about achievements, the latter statement at any rate is, I think, doubtfully true. What, following David McClelland, psychologists call 'N-Ach' ('Need for Achievement') can provide strong motives, though it may be for achievements in sport rather than in what are called 'higher things'. N-Ach postulates preparedness to maintain tensions in the interests of distant goals, and a disposition to compete with a standard of excellence which a person has set himself and for which he has an emotional concern.[9] Those lacking in it may lack, as we say, 'motivation'. They may escape some conflicts with social morality, but it would be odd to think of them as therefore the more moral. The stickler for social morality, on the other hand, may so exasperate the person set on achievement as to encourage him to think that he should put himself beyond good and evil. He may do so the more readily by taking an escape route from what might be considered to be duties to other people by seeing social morality as, at best, custom, and, at worst, as the Existentialists would say, bad faith, or, as with Nietzsche, a way in which weak and little people try to protect themselves against strong and big people. I have said that these are inadequate views of social morality, but even on a more adequate view the tension can still be there, and have the stuff of tragedy in it.

I have here been taking 'purity of heart' as single-mindedness, but this again may be an inadequate view. If, therefore, 'purity of heart' is taken as single-mindedness, we cannot say that it wills 'the good' without qualification, unless 'the good' is defined tautologically as that which one whole-heartedly wills. Single-mindedness may be a blinkered vision, whereas 'purity of heart' may be a condition for clarity achieved after heart-searching over moral complexities, where it cannot be taken for granted that one thing should always be given priority. The Existentialist emphasis on morality as free individual choice, and the teleological view of devotion to an exclusive project, both leave behind as a casualty the accommodations of social morality. What in fact is being left behind? Is it a restriction to escape from, or is it an arrangement of common affairs which may support individual creative efforts, and which itself needs to contain creative elements if it is to be viable? Or is it both of these?

In fact, not many people can live from a purely internal urge to do one thing and express their creativity by insulating themselves from social relationships, except in so far as these can be bent to serve their overriding dedication. In more cases, the ability to do creative work comes from a meeting of inner flair and outward need, opportunity, and, in fortunate cases, the finding of a role. This does not solve the moral problem of priorities, but it makes it less likely for such people that their relationships with others will be ignored except in so far as they can be used to serve a central aim. We come back, therefore, from the morality of single-minded dedication to one such aim, to the complexity which also looks at the social setting in which it is followed. If we can get a more adequate view of social morality, those who reject it in the name of something else to which they give priority can at least see better what it is that they are rejecting.

11 Social Morality Reconsidered[1]

That social morality needs to contain creative elements if it is to be viable, has, I think, been distorted by the dominant sociological picture. Here we see *Homo sociologicus* as one who plays roles according to rules, and conforms to norms, or is brought back from deviation, by social pressures. Even as an abstract model, this is inadequate, if we have regard to facts of conflict and change as well as to those of consensus and conformity. In reality, roles are played with individual style; rules are bent to fit difficult cases, and bending them can sometimes be a moral and not an immoral way of behaving, unless morality is simply defined as obedience to the rules. Much of life is not morally programmed; there are situations where rules as well as roles may conflict; and they may not be a sure guide in times of change. In other words, we cannot escape the need for imagination, sensitivity, judgement—the spirit of Aristotle's *phronimos*, the man of practical wisdom. Nearly everyone knows this and innumerable people have considerable skill in practising it. If they did not, social morality would be far too stereotyped to work even as well as it does. So, since life itself puts one into situations of changing circumstances and of conflicts of obligations, a programmed stereotypy would not even be viable as a social morality. A viable social morality is not just a single line marked out by rules; it needs to be seen as something more like a three-stranded cord. 'Three strands' suggest intertwining, and not just triple threads. A three-fold cord is not easily broken; and if social morality is to stand the strains of actual life, I believe it will need at least these three strands, though sociologists and moral philosophers and some religious people have all too often tried to talk as if a sufficient account could be given in terms of one of them, while the others can be discarded or allotted to some other concern.[2]

I shall call the first strand 'Custom' and the second 'Reciprocity'. There is no obvious name for the third. I shall call it
'Generosity', as expressing a humane, outgoing imagination in
moral dealings, which may, but need not necessarily, have a
religious root.³ I shall label these three strands C, R, and G, for
convenience of reference. From time to time I shall talk about C,
R, and G types of moral behaviour. But this must not be taken to
mean that an all-round working morality can fall under one of
these types as if it were self-sufficient. They need each other, just
as the people who chiefly rely on one of them will need people who
rely on the others. And though people may 'major' in one, I doubt
whether anyone's morality can belong *solely* to one type. Sociologists have tried to talk about morality purely in C terms, moral
philosophers in R terms, some religious people in G terms, but
this is abstraction, not life in the round.

First, then, C—Custom. 'Custom' stands broadly for the *mores*,
the morality which is a going—or not so going—concern in any
society. It is a mixture of rules of thumb, wisdom of experience,
and taboos whose original point, if any, may have been forgotten.
It may not fit well into existing situations, especially when times
are changing. But whether we conform or whether we revolt, we
all depend more than we like to own on there being some persist-
ing customs which will give us reasonably stable expectations as
to how other people are likely to behave, and saving us from
always having to think out how we ourselves should behave all
along the line. We need to be able to take a good deal for granted
on some occasions, if we are to have the energy to think, criticise,
and innovate on others. So we need custom as well as spontaneity,
and this can be seen even in the 'alternative societies' set up by
people who repudiate the existing *mores*. They very soon have to
produce *mores* of their own, or else their communes peter out in
uncertainty and instability. In any case, they count on some fairly
constant framework being kept going in the wider society out of
which they have partially contracted—at any rate they expect to
find road and rail transport and telephone communications.

It may be said that all this is sociologically interesting: that
'Custom is King' may even be part of what is meant by a society.
But what has it to do with morality? Morality should be a matter
of people's free personal decisions on what they think right or
wrong: the *mores* are only moral where they are deliberately
accepted. This is partly a matter of definition. We can, if we like,

call the customary element just 'social behaviour', and reserve 'morality' for people's deliberate decisions about what they ought to do, and this is how most moral philosophers in our culture would take it. What is not a matter of definition, but of fact, is that first-hand decisions are exacting and often time-consuming. We often have to act off the cuff, and fall back on built-in dispositions which have been formed out of intuitively absorbed social training as well as out of our own former decisions. Existentialists speak as though morality should consist of agonising choices, where there are no guidelines, and where we must act in absolute freedom. So indeed it sometimes does, but it can hardly do so all the time; there are too many decisions to be made in the course of the day. If in most of them we fall back on customary guidelines, the Existentialists will call this *'mauvaise foi'*. Then we shall have to carry a great load of inevitable guilt feelings along with us, and this is a grim prospect. We can, of course, give general assent to some of the rules we find round us in the *mores* (though 'general assent' would not satisfy an Existentialist). If we cannot give (or withold) assent in personal reflection all along the line, often the best we can hope for is that the parts of the *mores* which we still take for granted will not be too indefensible, and that our failure to be self-conscious about them will not land us into serious *mauvaise foi*. But I am not happy about excluding from social morality even the parts of the *mores* which we have not examined and consented to, because if we do exclude them, we may well not have the honesty and humility to acknowledge how often we depend on them. So it may be better to bring this above board, and allow custom (whether consciously or tacitly accepted) to be one strand—though only one—in our actual working social morality. Some customs are not just what we ourselves would have prescribed if we had thought them up. But I do not see how a society can cohere without a good deal that can be taken for granted in this way. Karl Popper's 'open society' inhabited by pure critical rationalists would not, I suspect, cohere for very long.[4] Social morality runs a good deal on custom; and we are being less than candid about our own personal behaviour unless we own that we rely to a very considerable extent on rules of thumb to which we give little or no critical attention.

For this very reason the customary side of morality can let us down. For we are faced with situations to which the *mores* have not been tailored; even parts of them thought to be 'self-evident intuitions' may turn out not so self-evident to a later generation. Also the *mores* are a mixed bag; some of them got there through good sense born of experience, and some in much more chancy ways. How do we tell the difference?

We can try to do so by using our wits, critically as to consequences, and with a sense of fairness as a guiding light as to principle. This brings us to R, the second strand, which I have labelled Reciprocity. Broadly this attempts to bring some rationality into customary morality. As one of our strands, I believe it is present in what are thought of as traditional societies, where a good deal of shrewd comment goes on. But of course, it is more noticeable in societies where people are learning to think critically, and where traditional moral sanctions are loosened. It is therefore the approach distinctive of liberal moral reformers.

The R strand in morality, then, is produced by reflecting on the mixed set of customs which make up the C strand. If reflection is to be critical, it needs a guiding light, and I have called this strand the R strand because the main guiding light is Reciprocity. This can cover both a sense of fairness and mutual respect for interests and obligations. If being 'rational' is not only to be defined in prudential terms, as maximising one's own interests on a cost-benefit basis, it can be extended into seeing that if one expects other people to keep a rule it is only fair to be prepared to do so oneself. This means 'treat alike cases which are alike in the relevant respect'. The rationality of consistency can, of course, go along with a conservative view of the rules. But even this tells us not to cheat over the rules in our favour—a first step into rational objectivity, and one not to be despised. Taken along with mutual respect for interests, this minimum fairness can grow beyond merely seeing that we should not make exceptions in our own favour into a more imaginative kind of reciprocity, a capacity to think of oneself as in the other man's shoes, and see how the situation would look if the roles were reversed (especially in a non-symmetrical transaction where one of the parties is the under-dog at the receiving end). Reciprocity, then, points not only to consistent morality but to Golden Rule morality.

Consistency and mutual respect: this sounds very Kantian, and indeed Kant might be taken as the paradigm philosopher of the R strand. But even Kant, when he is talking *morality* and not just doing meta-ethics, brings in some actual notions of right and wrong taken out of the *mores* of the Protestant Christianity in which he was brought up. Nevertheless, broadly speaking, Kant's morality is the R strand, a morality of rational beings, treating each other as such with impartial natural justice. It is the kind of morality that we hold should underlie uncorrupt administrative and judicial procedures. It operates without respect of persons, but with respect *for* persons, an essential distinction where impersonal decisions are called for.

This impersonality may be why it has a bad press in some contemporary circles, notably those connected with the 'counter-culture', where 'bureaucrat' has become a dirty word, with 'soul-less' as something of an inseparable prefix. Here not only the C strand of the *mores* is suspect, but also the R strand; the liberal effort after fairness and rationality. But not so the G strand, generous action of a directly personal kind. This stands partly for the quest for an elusive ideal which cannot be contained in any set of rules. Rules, if they are not just arbitrarily imposed by some people on other people, go with the morality of Reciprocity. You accept the fact that if you expect other people to keep them, then you should do so too in cases when they apply to you. And correspondingly, if you are to be expected to keep them, then you most certainly hold that other people ought to do so too. Otherwise your readiness to keep them will become strained, to say the least; in any case Reciprocity embraces a morality of give and take.

The G morality is not thus calculating, however fair and reasonable such calculations may be. It stands for a highly personal kind of behaviour, which certainly cannot be prescribed in any set of rules, or be expected as of right. At one end of the scale, this is the morality of saints and heroes; but there is a scale, and there are points all up it where it comes out in the behaviour of all sorts of people, in uncovenanted, gracious acts of kindness where people are prepared, freely and ungrudgingly, not always to stand on their rights.

How does this connect with institutional morality? In institutional behaviour we need to know more or less where we stand and what we can reasonably expect and fairly demand of each other. The Sermon on the Mount contains sayings which are paradigmatic pieces of G morality. But 'Give, hoping for nothing again' is hardly a principle on which a Joint Stock Bank could run; nor 'Judge not that ye be not judged' be the appropriate maxim for members of appointments committees. The drop-outs who want all our transactions to be directly personal and spontaneous over-look the fact that many of them involve a range of obligations to others beyond immediate face-to-face individuals; and some of these transactions—appointing to a job, for instance—call for attempts at impartial assessing of relevant qualities, if justice is to be done both to the candidates who do not get the job and to those who are going to have to live with the candidate who does. This does not mean that the qualities so estimated are necessarily the most important, though it is hoped that they are the ones which are relevant to the situation. In any case, behind and beyond them stands the actual individual person, and confronted with him 'Judge not' may strike the appropriate note. Yet since we are involved in innumerable transactions in multiple relations, most of which have to be indirect, we depend on some institutional framework in which they can be structured. And if there is to be some institutional framework, it is surely preferable to try to bring R principles to bear on it—reciprocity tempered by reason—rather than just to trust to the folk-ways, which left to themselves can well be custom tempered by corruption.

This does not mean that people with roles in institutions in which they try to behave in a R-like way can have no time for the G kind of behaviour. Just as G cannot stand by itself as a social morality, because it would produce anarchy,[5] so R needs a touch of inspired innovation as well as compassion if it is not to lead to the 'soul-less bureaucracy' which the drop-out thinks it is. This is not just a way of saying that bureaucrats may after all have a soul in their off-duty moments. It is to say that even in their on-duty moments, when making decisions according to rules and prece-dents, there is a difference between knowing and not knowing that they are also doing things with people's lives. And many of them do know it. A wise administrator knows that any set of rules needs loopholes. But they must be loopholes. The drop-out who repudi-ates institutional decisions sometimes seems to be asking for the loophole to be made into the rule. But if what is done through the loophole is made into a new rule, it may be still less workable than the old one. It is broadly true that hard cases make bad laws. In any case, the genius of the G kind of morality lies in seeing when the rule is no longer the guide.

Less drastic than finding loopholes, there is also the fact that no system of rules can be administered without some place for discre-tion, and G can come out in the use of discretion. I once considered dedicating something I wrote remotely connected with this theme to 'administrators whose hearts are with the anarchists, and to anarchists who have a heart for the administrators'. I do not think that the former at any rate are a null class. The pure Weberian model of impersonal rule-governed rational bureaucracy is far too pure to exist. In any case, if it did exist it would soon be strangled in its own red tape. For the role of administrator, like all roles, is not simply a matter of applying rules. Cases are too varied for all decisions to be so programmed. There is the question of which rule applies and how; there are exceptional circumstances; there is the penumbra of personal relationships which surround even rather formal kinds of transaction. There has to be a margin for discretion, and the individual plays his role in his own style, more and less humanely.

This gives a foothold for G qualities, even in quite routine kinds of transaction. At a simple level they can come out in courtesy and patience, which indeed can come to be expected in a civilised society. I was in a small branch Post Office in Manchester when an elderly pensioner in front of me was drawing his pension, and getting into muddles which the woman behind the counter was gently sorting out for him. This much might be expected from a Post Office employee, and the public might well complain if they were treated brusquely. But it was not all. After the old man had gone, the woman behind the counter said to me 'They do get into muddles. But we know our pensioners, and if they haven't been in for three weeks, one of us slips round to where they live to see if they are all right.' Note 'our pensioners'. And since some of them might well be living alone, and not able to get out if they were ill, I should not be surprised if the woman from the Post Office not only took along their pension, but did a bit of clearing up and shopping for them as well—an unobtrusive bit of G behaviour beyond the duties of her role.

Yet within the duties of the role there is the place for the attitude of mind in which the role-player carries them out, and this comes out in administration even at a simple level. The higher the level, the more the administrator is likely to be faced with problems and conflicts of moral considerations, where neither custom nor rule will be enough. Those whose capacities, intellectual as well as moral, are not equal to such conflicts are likely to relapse in a confusion of inconsistent expediencies, or in the end break down. Their view of morality may have been too simple; a more complex view can combine with moral toughness to enable a person to face conflicts and re-define situations so as to perceive possible solutions not allowed for on a more stereotyped view.[6] The higher the level, therefore, the more necessary it may be that the people who have these responsibilities should be able to feel the pull of the G strand of morality, even if their job mainly asks them to keep the R strand in repair.

Similarly, if those who run mainly on the C strand of custom are not just to turn into programmed conformists, they will need the occasional inspired innovation, and the far less occasional touch of spontaneous imagination, which comes from the spirit of G. Beyond these again are the heroic, sacrificial kinds of G action. But G also may go to the bad, if it is taken as self-sufficient. The horrible possibilities of what might happen here were borne in on me at an early age when I came across a Victorian children's book that had belonged to my mother. It was about two little girls who never quarrelled except about which of them should give up. They were obviously each wanting to be in the superior moral position of the giver-up, and the book unintentionally showed me that it was much better for most of family life to run on principles of give and take and fair shares. Most, but not all; sometimes people indeed need to be prepared to give and not take. The hopeless thing about the little girls in the story was that they wanted to make this into a rule, and since it was a rule that *both* of them could not keep at the same time, they had to quarrel over it. Also they did not have the humility to see that one must sometimes be the taker.

There is another reason why there are dangers in trying to run life on G considerations alone, and this is shown where morality goes along with aspiration after an extreme ideal. Seekers after an extreme ideal will be exasperated by the compromises of give and take. And when they are exasperated, the sacrificial drive in their morality can turn to violence. For violence can also be sacrificial, since those who take to it know they are as likely—often more likely—to be killed as to kill. Violence is the dark shadow of sacrificial morality, which may be why people who live by this morality are more able to talk to the violent than are the liberal people who live mainly by the R principles of Reciprocity.

I have separated C, R, and G because people's morality can predominantly belong to one of these rather than the others. But I have questioned whether any one of them can exist on its own.

The G person needs some customs to fall back on; and if he is not prepared to run some of his transactions on the reciprocity of give and take, he will wear us all out and end up as a fanatic. And I have spoken of how C and R types need the touch of G to give them creative imagination and personal compassion, to counter the drag to complacency and conformity.

The distinction of C, R, and G strands is but one possible distinction within morality seen as an essentially contestable concept. Another distinction to which I have already drawn attention is that between factors of principle, purpose and approval, emphasised theoretically in the deontological, teleological and axiological types of moral view. In so far as the behaviour with which I have been concerned in this chapter is that of the social morality of mutual dealings between people who stand in a great variety of relations to one another, the C, R, and G distinction could be seen as falling within a broadly deontological morality of interpersonal obligations. But in so far as such social morality is guided by a concern to maintain, perhaps improve, perhaps also change, the common life of a community, it will also have a teleological aspect of purpose; and whether we try to maintain, or to improve, or to change, or even to subvert, will depend on what kind of community we approve of as one in which we would want to live. Just as each type of moral theory emphasises a factor which cannot in fact stand alone, though it may well be seen as dominant, so too practical social morality needs to be seen as a complex of more than one factor. If it includes imaginative judgement guiding discretion, it is more than a set of customs, or even a set of principles, however liberal.

Yet, however rich and complex it may be, social morality is not the whole of morality. There is also the morality internal to a person's own life-style, particularly where his desire to 'do his own thing' is an effort to do something of a creative kind. If single-minded devotion to an exclusive aim can make life ruthless, social morality alone can make it banal.

The person who is seriously trying to see where his social duty lies needs not a daemonic spirit, but the imagination and inner resistance to mere convention which were its strength. The person struggling to follow his own creative purpose needs social morality if only to deal with the pull towards self-centredness which can come from the assertion of his own powers. And not only social morality; he needs also self-knowledge. The person who tries to put himself beyond good and evil in the sense of social morality may not only scorn this morality but be too proud for self-knowledge. The person who has developed a first-hand conscience, through seriously trying to make moral judgements in his dealings with other people, may not only come to self-knowledge, but may achieve a capacity for trained intuitive judgement.

This is not simple moralism, nor the notion of moral intuition of self-evident duties. It is discernment as a practical skill, where there is neither axiomatic nor deductive certainty. It is creativity in moral judgement.

12 Towards the Sovereignty of Good

Practical wisdom calls for informed judgement, discerning emphases to be given to different features within morality seen as an essentially contestable concept, where no one feature can be assumed to have undisputed priority. We have seen that those who claim to be 'beyond good and evil' are likely to define morality in terms of one such factor, and then see it as a moralism to be superseded for the sake of something more important. The aesthetic way of life came nearest to producing an amoral alternative, without commitment to purpose or principle, accepting the world as spectacle, and judging actions as giving or failing to give aesthetic satisfaction.

Morality indeed calls for powers of appreciation, to see what people are like in their passions, conflicts, achievements, and here the arts of the novelist and poet, sometimes too the painter, can enlarge understanding. But beyond understanding, morality is turned towards action, to principles which guide it and to purposes to be achieved, and to the clashes of principle and purpose, of principle and principle, and of purpose and purpose. There are diversities of claims, and priorities cannot be assumed.

Different types of theory may indeed give prominence to one feature rather than another, but a serious theory must, I believe, recognise that all have a place in any possible morality. 'Any possible morality.' The phrase suggests a moral pluralism, even if a limited one.[1] The kind of pluralism at issue is not just the diversity of *mores*, of different local codes, the old story of cultural relativism.

> There are nine and sixty ways of constructing tribal lays,
> And every single one of them is right[2]

Contemporary anthropologists are less disposed than their founding fathers to find this extreme pluralism. The latter were no

125

doubt also taking pleasure in knocking Victorian moralism. In 1907, W. G. Sumner, writing about the *mores* (a term he coined) taught that the *mores* can make anything right. In 1955, Robert Redfield commented (quoting Robert E. Park) that 'the *mores* have a harder time making some things right than others'.[3] Diversity in *mores* is often dubbed 'relativism', a vague notion within which we can distinguish hard and soft forms. 'Hard Relativism' would be a view that moral notions are causally dependent on something else in a culture—its inter-familial relationships, for instance, or its economic or power structure. 'Soft Relativism' would be the view that there can indeed be distinctive moral interests, but the form taken by the moral practices which implement them can be affected by other factors within the culture. I find the soft form more plausible. However, my concern here is not with diversity in *mores*, but with diversity in types of moral theory, reflecting different emphases. There is nothing new in the notion of a diversity of types. James Martineau wrote *Types of Ethical Theory* in 1885, and C. D. Broad wrote *Five Types of Ethical Theory* in 1930, and their types are by no means exhaustive. Is this diversity limited by there being certain necessary conditions for any possible morality, even if no one is a sufficient defining condition?

One candidate has been Universalisability. To be moral is to accept that what would be right for you would be right for me if similarly placed. This goes with giving reasons for what may be right, since a reason, as distinct from an emotional reaction, must be more general than the immediate instance. Universalisability, however, cannot be a sufficient criterion of morality, since it only tells us to be consistent in the use of principles, not what principles to adopt. If we are prepared to say that anyone who applies his principles consistently is *ipso facto* moral, we can be confronted with what R. M. Hare calls 'fanatics': his example is the non-Jew who says that it is right to gas Jews because he sincerely maintains that he himself, were he a Jew, ought to be gassed. Hare thinks such people are logically unassailable. But he shows he is uneasy by calling them 'fanatics'. 'Fanatics' is a term of opprobrium, and thus brings in an axiological factor. It suggests that this very consistency in applying these principles can be a menace. Hare does indeed now supplement the notion of morality as consistency in the application of one's chosen principles with a notion of regard for interests.[4] A person's interests can be described not just as anything he happens to want, but as those conditions which will increase his opportunities of getting what he wants, where his 'wants' are reasonably steady, and not just episodic (Hare speaks of 'prudent' desires). The means-end connotation in 'interests' brings a teleological factor into what is otherwise a deontological morality of principles, and Hare shows this in calling his more recent view a form of Utilitarianism. In a recent paper, 'Ethical Theory and Utilitarianism'[5] he says people can be asked if they would universalise the disregarding of interests if this included their own, and if not, whether they should disregard the interests of other people. This can take care of selfishness. Hare thinks that it can also take care of the 'fanatic', if he is prepared to give everybody else's ideals equal consideration with his own, and still believes that, impartially weighed, the intensity of his desired ideal would outweigh the rest. Then if the fanatic is to come within the scheme, he must be required to have a judicial attitude towards his own ideals, which is just what he will not have, *qua* fanatic, one might say by definition. Hare can say that it is only if fanatics are prepared so to universalise, and still hold that their ideal has precedence, that they are a logical trouble to him. This may be; but if this judicial attitude towards their own ideals goes with a kind of moral psychology that fanatics would only have by ceasing to be fanatics, they should still be a moral trouble to him, since they would be impervious to his scheme of argument. The switch from talking about 'interests' to talking about 'ideals', which can be passionate rather than 'prudent' desires, underlines this.

'Ideals' are nevertheless moral factors, and not all ideals need be held fanatically. My present concern is with the fact that notions such as 'interests' and 'ideals' bring a teleological factor into what would otherwise, with its emphasis on Universalisability, be a morality of principles. Principles, if they are not seen as self-authenticating, or as pure matters of choice, can be codifications of basic approvals, and can also be supplemented by reference to the purposes they promote. Moreover, there are principles and principles. If morality were just a matter of consistency in applying principles, it would be rigorist, blinkered, or just plain silly.

Indeed, if we look at the greatest moral theory which centred on the notion of principle, namely Kant's, we see that, while it says that one should act on a maxim which one can will to be a universal law, it says more than just 'Be consistent', or even 'Do not adopt self-defeating maxims such as that everyone should tell lies'. Besides the dominant deontological factor that one should do one's duty according to principle, there is a latent axiological factor; some principles could not be *willed* because they would be conducive to a society of which one could not approve, such as one in which people acted on the principle of not bothering to improve their talents; although there need be nothing self-contradictory in adopting such a principle, Kant says one could not *will* this as a universal law.

Universalisability, as consistency in the application of principles, then, can be backed by approval of the principles to be applied and the purposes which they serve. Where do we look for criteria of approvals? One simple answer is the emotivist's; one need not look further than one's own feelings, expressed in one's 'pro-' and 'con-' attitudes. But a *judgement* of approval, if one acknowledges a need to justify it to others, or indeed to justify it to oneself, must be more than just expression of feeling. If justification is to be more than rationalising the feelings one already has, it will appeal for corroboration by others or by oneself in a cool hour, and it may be open to reconsideration.

One way of justifying or of revising approvals and deciding whether they are *moral* approvals was suggested by Adam Smith. The appeal is to the verdict of the character he called 'the Impartial Spectator'; recent moralists have appealed to a more rarefied character called 'the Ideal Observer'. For Adam Smith, approval of the attitude of another person and the conduct stemming from it comes from sympathy, sympathy being 'a fellow feeling with any passion of another whatsoever'. ('Sympathy' in this use is concordance *with* the passions of another, not a feeling for another.) Though this feeling is at the root of moral sentiment, as a moral sentiment it must be combined with a sense of the *propriety* of the passion, particularly as being or not being in proportion to its cause. A passion of violent anger, for instance, might be disproportionate to the cause which excites it. 'Propriety' brings in an element of judgement besides feeling, and it is the approval of the 'Impartial Spectator' stemming from this which should be the court of appeal. Adam Smith's Impartial Spectator, 'the man within the breast', stands for the capacity to distance oneself from one's own emotions and conduct; to see how they would look from another point of view, perhaps from what would nowadays be called a 'reversal of roles', though the Impartial Spectator does not necessarily give the verdict from the reversed role. He gives his verdict impartially.

The considerations Adam Smith's Impartial Spectator takes into account are very much those of eighteenth-century British educated society. Though Adam Smith was not a Utilitarian, 'utility' has an important place in justifying his Impartial Spectator's approval. He approves of mutually supporting actions which make part of 'a system of behaviour which tends to promote the happiness either of the individual or of the society'; our approval of such utility would be as when 'we approve of a convenient and well-contrived building', an aesthetic pleasure in the 'beauty of utility'. This becomes moral in so far as the spectator, or the agent turning himself into spectator, takes account of the 'propriety' of the emotion expressed in the action in relation to its cause, and the 'merit', which here means whether it is held to deserve praise or blame in view of its beneficial or hurtful consequences to others. All this sounds very eighteenth-century, especially in the emphasis on the 'amiable' virtues. There could be the notion of an Impartial Spectator who would be 'the man within the breast', giving the verdict of the internalised conscience of moral values of a different sort. Dr Thomas Campbell has called the Impartial Spectator 'an empirical ideal type'.[6] If he is not just the internalised super-ego of a particular social group, he represents the kind of man that someone living in such a society would like to be.

Adam Smith's Impartial Spectator has eighteenth-century tastes, guiding his approvals or disapprovals by the way conduct promotes or disturbs social harmony and affects people's happiness or unhappiness. When the 'Ideal Observer' comes on the scene in the works of some contemporary moralists, he is a much more austere figure, far from any empirically recognisable type. Professor Firth[7] has defined an Ideal Observer as one who would know all the facts, could visualise the consequences of all possible alternative actions, and was impartial, in not being influenced by particular interests ('particular' here meaning designated by proper names). Such an Ideal Observer would surely have to be God. Professor Brandt indeed tries to make him a more possibly human figure. He must be sane, possessed of correct beliefs on any facts relevant to any ethical point at issue in a maximally clear and vivid form, not be ill, not in a condition of physical craving,

fatigued, excited, nor depressed, and have a strong and favourable sentiment towards all human beings, and no biasing towards
particular groups or statuses.[8] This comes nearer to a possible
human observer, but still an ideal rather than an actual one, as
indeed the name of the theory acknowledges. What would it be
like to have clear beliefs on all the relevant facts in a maximally
clear and vivid form? The requirement that he be impartial, in
that his reactions would be similar in all situations where people
have the same relevant properties, is of course the Universalisability criterion transcribed from principles into approvals. He must
also, Brandt says, have a strong and favourable sentiment towards
all human beings. This is indeed an attitude of mind which an
actual observer might cultivate, but he could never be sure he had
it in a maximum degree. Nevertheless, the appeal to the judgement of an Ideal Observer could be an appeal to what Kantians
would call a Regulative Ideal. The attempt to approximate to it
could guide judgement; one can become sensitive to deviations
from it, though one cannot say except in abstract terms what it
would be like to satisfy it completely.

When we come to actual moral judgements which we imagine
might be made by Ideal Observers, these may well vary according
to the moral surround in which they are passed. By this I do not
just mean the empirical cultural moral surround. I mean rather
the reactions of an Ideal Observer could be affected by the type of
moral theory he is supposed to hold. The approvals of an
Utilitarian Ideal Observer might not be the same as those of a
Kantian one, or those of a more aesthetically-minded, whom I
shall call a 'Nietzschean', one. So while the appeal to an Ideal
Observer fastens on the factor of approval guided by impartiality
and knowledge of facts, these do not provide sufficient moral
criteria, since 'believing correctly all the facts' which would make
a difference to his reaction, even if it could be known that he did
so, would not in itself produce a unique moral reaction. Facts and
their consequences have to be evaluated, and if he is to evaluate
(let alone evaluate uniquely) the Ideal Observer will need some
further qualifications. Brandt does indeed also give his Ideal
Observer a strong and favourable sentiment towards all human
beings, and this attitude of benevolence might evaluate facts in
their bearing on people's welfare or happiness. Brandt's Ideal
Observer, with disinterestedness, knowledge of facts and general
benevolence, might be a universal utilitarian of the Sidgwick type,

one who would consider consequences in their effect on people's welfare and happiness, and would also have a sense of fairness. There could still, however, be the question, for instance, of how an Ideal Observer would evaluate the priorities of someone striving for excellence in some particular attainment which may cut across concern for other people's welfare. There might also be a Kantian Ideal Observer, in whom the attitude of general benevolence gave place to one of respect for people's moral nature and moral freedom. Such a Kantian Ideal Observer need not take his stand on the notion of inviolate moral principles; there is a more liberal Kantian position, where the categorical imperative stands for confronting another person as a rational moral being. This Kantian Ideal Observer would not be concerned with the consequences for human welfare of a person's behaviour, but with seeing whether it expresses a good will. There might also be a Nietzschean Ideal Observer, who would approve of whatever led to someone doing something important, 'important' standing, for instance, for some intellectual or aesthetic achievement, not necessarily just for the advancement of power. He could approve of other people being used for this, if the end was judged sufficiently important.

Here are three different types of Ideal Observer, registering approvals in the context of three different types of moral theory, and there could indeed be more. All Ideal Observers, however, share the quality of impartiality, and, in whatever moral surround they figure, they may all be taken to disapprove of callousness. By callousness, I mean indifference where care and thought could be taken. This is not the same as freedom from emotional involvement in circumstances where in fact there is nothing one can do. This—a form of Stoic *apatheia*—may indeed in some circumstances be a condition of moral and social survival.

Universalisability, then, as consistency of principle and impartiality in judgement, is by no means a sufficient moral criterion. Some Ideal Observer theorists put more flesh on these bones by adding a quality of general benevolence, but this is not incontestable. Moreover, are the original criteria of consistency and impartiality incontestable? If not sufficient criteria of moral judgements, are they even necessary ones? Consistency demands that what would be a reason in one situation would also be a reason in others like it. But Existentialists would say that there will never be anyone just like me, or any other situation just like this one. So I must make my unique decision, for which no reasons can be given, since reasons in the nature of the case are couched in general terms. This would cut out *thinking* about what one ought to do. A decision would be an individual response to a situation with no reasons by which one could back or justify it. Sometimes, no doubt, we may be reduced to these desperate straits, but I doubt whether they are prototypic of all serious moral decisions.

Nevertheless, there may well be situations where the moral decision has to be made not with an attitude of detached impartiality, but where one is, as the Existentialists would say, *engagé*. One is committed, or one is passionately on someone's side; one might be in a towering rage, and the very strength of one's feelings might produce a more inspired judgement than might have come out of judicial detachment. Current Universalisability and Ideal Observer theories use forensic metaphors; the substantive virtues built into them are the judicial virtues.[9] What is put forward as a piece of meta-ethics is in fact a part of a theory (or can appear as a part of various theories) which also has normative implications and whose generality over the whole range of moral judgements can be disputed.

Another suggested distinguishing characteristic of morality is that it is binding; the moral 'ought', as distinct from the deliberative 'ought' and as distinct from inclination, has binding force. If this is not just to be social pressure, it must be a pressure one puts on oneself. R. M. Hare puts this in an extreme way by saying that the force of 'ought' is that of a command, and that 'I ought to do this' is a command which I address to myself.

Small children are indeed sometimes found telling themselves to do and not to do things, probably because they are imitating what their elders say to them. But in adult life one does not usually so talk to oneself. In any case, why should an adult tell himself to do things unless he has some reason for doing so? And in communications to other people sheer command is hardly a basis for moral obedience, unless there is some context in which it is held that the person commanding is entitled to be obeyed.

The morally prescriptive 'ought' is, therefore, not just a command. I have suggested that its force may come from a commitment.[10] Commitment is here being used widely, where there have been previous resolutions, or even where one has set oneself towards a way of living which will have implications for one's later actions. (I am not here thinking of intellectual commitments to

particular views, expect in so far as these have practical consequences.) Contracts are a paradigm case of commitments carrying obligations—so too are promises, but in the case of contracts
the obligation is a mutual one. Some moralists have therefore tried
to present the 'obligation' aspect of morality in a contract model.
Russell Grice, in *The Grounds of Moral Judgment* (Cambridge, 1967)
derives what he calls basic obligations from the proposition that
there is something which it is in some sense in everyone's interest
that everyone should be required to do; and this implies that it is
in everyone's interest to place himself under an obligation to do
this provided everyone else does so too. This is represented as
contractually placing the requirements on oneself.[11] (Grice has a
character whom he calls 'The Master Criminal' who sees that the
existence of such a contract is in his interest, as prescribing how
people in general should behave, though he has his own ways of
evading his part in it. There is nothing much to be done about the
Master Criminal except to try and stop him.) John Rawls has also
presented a model of Justice, as defining an agreement to abide by
arrangements which would be accepted as fair by reasonable
people in an original position in which everyone is put under a
'veil of ignorance' whereby he is precluded from knowing what he
personally might stand to lose or gain.[12] This has analogies with
contract theories, but the weight is carried by the notion of what
rational men might agree to, and not by the notion of a putative
undertaking.

The appeal of contract theories, especially where some putative
social contract is made the basis of moral as well as political
obligation, is that it seems unreasonable to say that one has
obligations which one has in no sense undertaken; and, moreover,
the mutual undertaking in the notion of a contract suggests a
reason for making it—would an undertaking be mutual if it were
not to the interest of both parties? In the case of moral obligations,
how far can this notion of mutual undertaking be stretched
metaphorically to cover cases where there is no explicit agreement
between parties or means of enforcement?' While a contract is a
paradigm example of a commitment, I should want to use the
notion of commitment more widely to cover not only mutual
undertakings, but the taking on of courses of action or adoption of
principles consequent on one's considered way of life. One can
thus keep the element of responsible acceptance without having to
imagine mutual undertakings. Particular obligations can then be

consequential on this acceptance, rather than each one severally being taken account of *de novo* as something to be accepted or rejected. This need not mean, however, that we are just saddled with them.

Undoubtedly a good many of our 'obligations' do seem to be things we just find ourselves saddled with: this may be because they are part of the *mores*—we are socialised into thinking we should so behave, and this, we have seen, is a source of the unanalysed feeling of 'ought'. Where the 'ought' is what I have called a pressure we put on ourselves in virtue of a commitment, and where this commitment is not an explicit mutual undertaking, it can be seen more generally as consequent on one's considered decision to live in one way rather than another. So, though people are not responsible for having parents as they are for having children, they may, none the less, hold themselves to be committed to doing something about helping their parents in their old age. This is sometimes presented as a quasi-contractual return for services rendered in childhood. More likely, it is seen as part of a way of living in which one acquires concern for the needs of people with whom one has been intimately connected. This can be a concern which may not only be induced by social conditioning. It can become part of a responsibly adopted life-style. In making commitment, as distinct from unanalysed pressure, stand behind 'ought', I am not saying that there need be no reasons for commitments, still less that to what one is committed does not matter so long as one is committed (which seems sometimes implied in the Existentialist notion of engagement), and that one does not have sometimes to disengage oneself.

Commitment, therefore, though a factor in morality, cannot stand as a sufficient one. The more we recognise different factors within morality, and do not allow that priorities can always be settled by applying one of them across the board, the more the weight in making decisions has to rest on *judgement*. If judgement is not just to be snap, it must be capable of improvement, of there being good judgement as well as poor judgement. How then is it cultivated? Partly, like any skill, by exercise; by seeing that situations present problems, and struggling with what one ought to do where there are no textbook answers. Partly also by taking responsibility for a decision when made, and, if it turns out badly, trying to see what one can learn from it. Knowledge of facts is obviously part of this; and also a moral quality of disinterestedness, which may be deeper than the quality of judical impartiality which can be its appropriate form in some circumstances. This disinterestedness may be better designated as 'liberty of spirit', or even as the 'purity of heart' which Kierkegaard said was the condition for willing 'the Good'.

I have been speaking of 'moral judgements'. In the rest of this chapter I shall look at what it might mean for a moral judgement to be oriented towards 'good'. Is there a sense in which 'good' has pride of place, standing over principle, purpose and approvals, which may be variably emphasised in any given applications of the essentially contestable concept of morality? Whichever factor is emphasised, is it still subject to the sovereignty of good, so that it is no accident that the great amoralists seek to go 'beyond Good and Evil'?

I have borrowed the title of this chapter from Iris Murdoch's Leslie Stephen Lecture given in Cambridge in 1967—'The Sovereignty of Good over other Concepts'.[13] Miss Murdoch points to a latter-day Platonic Idea of the Good, which she says can guide our capacity to see things in their own right, in relation to what might be their own proper perfections. Such disinterested vision calls for detachment from self-centred egoism and possessiveness, and she calls it the mystical aspect of morality. Clarity of vision in art is an analogue; beauty in art, she says, can be goodness by proxy.[14]

How does the power to appreciate the character and potential perfections of individual things other than ourselves guide moral conduct, beyond freeing us, at least in the moment of vision, from wanting to bend them to our purposes? Such a way of seeing things in their own right may indeed have far-reaching importance, but there is much about morality which it does not say. It detaches us from purpose, but the notion of purpose has a place, even if not always an overriding place, in morality. Disinterested vision by itself could suggest Schopenhauer's way of escaping from the self-centred destructiveness of the will by its abnegation in a state of pure contemplation. Schopenhauer could also speak of this contemplation as good, but it is for him a good detached from moral notions of good and evil which belong to the illusory world of Maya. If we are left with pure relativism, if not illusion, in the good and evil of moral action, is there any reason to call this ultimate vision a vision of *good*, or should we call it a state of contemplative detachment beyond good and evil, linking it with aesthetics rather than morality?

This indeed could be said of Schopenhauer's vision. But Miss Murdoch is deeply concerned with morality. She looks towards an Idea of the Good beyond the particular perfections of individual things. Yet, as Aristotle said in criticising Plato's Idea of the Good, what does 'good' mean if it is not specifiable as good for a particular purpose or in a particular way?[15]

I shall come back to this, after looking at another approach—that of the prescriptivists, who would agree with the Oxford English Dictionary that 'good' is the most general adjective of commendation. This can go further than endorsing Hobbes' remark that 'Good and Evil signify only our appetites and aversions'. On the prescriptivist view we need not just be expressing likes and dislikes. We can be evincing certain options.

The crux is whether the opting is something for which justification can be given. Or can I only say that this is my choice, and I take responsibility for making it? To say this would obviously be congenial to Extentialists, and to say that this is all I mean by 'good' appears a modest claim. But to say that x is good sounds like commending it, which is why Charles Stevenson adds the rider 'Do so too' to 'I approve of x' as the analysis of 'x is good'.[16] But why should I approve of x because you tell me to? If you are bullying or cajoling me, why should I succumb, unless you can get me genuinely to share your approval? To say that something is better than something else in a specifiable context is to invoke the purposes and standards recognised in that context. One way to get you to share my approval is by getting you to see that you share or approve a purpose which x is said to promote, and then (Aristotle-wise) you can agree that x is good in that context. The context may be the social view of morality as a device by which people can live together through adopting certain principles of behaviour and encouraging certain attitudes which make them more likely to consider the interests of others besides themselves. John Mackie has a persuasive account of morality in these terms in his *Ethics: Inventing Right and Wrong* (Penguin, 1977). This is a subjective view in which morality is set up as a way of directing conduct, and is not in any way descriptive of fact. Within this device, there can be distinctions of 'better' and 'worse' compounded with reference to the function it serves. Mackie calls this social orientation a narrow sense of morality, as distinct from the wider sense in which morality, he says, would be whatever principles a person allows ultimately to determine his choices of action. Much of what he has to say about morality in the narrow sense shows practical wisdom, and something like it would need to be incorporated in any wider view. I am committed to using 'morality' in a wider sense, but not only as defined by Mackie in terms of principles, and therefore to trying to face the complexity which this involves. I cannot therefore restrict the moral use of 'better' and 'worse' to the context of devices within a social milieu. Nor can I give Mackie's form of subjectivism the last word. If I do not see moral terms as simply descriptive of fact, and yet do not believe that 'better' and 'worse' can only be used as consequent on our options and attitudes or as furthering a given purpose, I find myself wanting to invoke a notion of Good, in regulating their use.

To speak *simpliciter* of Good registers a conviction that there are things which are admirable which we can learn to appreciate, whether or not they further our interests and purposes, and, most importantly, that there can be growth in appreciation. One would like to say that Good is a Regulative Ideal to which one can approximate in saying 'x is better than y and y is better than x'. But for something to function as a Regulative Ideal one must know in principle what it would be like to satisfy it, even if it never in fact is satisfied, otherwise how do we know that we are getting nearer to it and when we are deviating from it? Since Good *simpliciter* is not specifiable as to its content, can one call its sovereignty over particular judgements of 'better and worse' a Regulative Ideal? I believe it has a function in standing for the belief that there can be growth in appreciation. To learn to appreciate is not just to register one's desires. It is to educate one's desires; to believe that judgements based on these at any given time can be improved; that one goes on learning, and that there is always likely to be a gap between what one appreciates here and now and what would be full appreciation. This would go for moral judgement as well as other kinds of appreciation such as aesthetic, and for our attempts to narrow the gap between what is subjectively right, as the best judgement one can now make, and what would indeed be the best judgement that could be made. Good, as what could command unqualified approval, is here used as a term with transcendental reference; we have met other such—'Objective Right', 'Will of God', 'verdict of an Ideal Observer'—and whether or not these have a metaphysical reference they function in affirming a belief that judgements are corrigible and there is indeed a difference between those which are better and those which are worse. 'Better and worse' would then not only register preferences, but be grounds for preference.

Grounds for preference can of course, often be specifiable within a recognised purpose, or with references to already existing desires. Since one can normally take for granted that a person does not want to get typhoid, if he is in an unhealthy place he can judge that it is better to boil his water and not just drink it out of the tap. Such cases are easy to defend. One could also easily defend the cases where a person is told that he will very likely enjoy something more, for instance a certain kind of beer, if he takes the trouble to try it on a number of occasions and to acquire the taste. The more difficult cases are where growth in appreciation does not reach this kind of end state. I have suggested that one may educate one's desires as well as one's judgements with reference to an ideal which will not be a particular finite end state at which one stops, and I have called such ideal notions 'transcendental'. Transcendental notions, if they meant that unless one occupies the transcendental position (which of course one does not) one cannot get going in making judgements, would stultify morality. The reference to them should set a direction; one must be able to get going in making moral judgements from where one is and also be able to say that there are ways of making them which can lead to improvement. Yet this marks out a direction of improvement, not the prospect of an achieved adequacy. The reference to a transcendental notion can have this function of indicating openness to a possibility which cannot be fully satisfied.

I have spoken of this as a process of learning to appreciate, and this brings in feelings as well as intellect. Here the 'axiological' aspect of morality comes to the fore, the aspect of morality as guided by our value judgements of approval and disapproval. If morality cannot be purely a matter of principles and purposes without these, then there is the question of whether they can be trained and modified through what we learn to appreciate.

To *learn to appreciate* presupposes something to be learnt. This is not just to say that we want things which will satisfy us, and had better find out what they are—either what will give most satisfaction or at least, in order to avoid trouble, what will give socially acceptable satisfaction. This was the position of the strict Benthamite Utilitarians, and led to the logical conclusion that, quantity of pleasure being equal, pushpin is as good as poetry. J. S. Mill tried (unsuccessfully on his premises) to maintain that some pleasures were qualitatively superior, on the dubious contention that the superior ones would afford more pleasure.[17] If this cannot be convincingly shown, at least as a general rule, then the argument for encouraging some ways of getting pleasure rather than others may turn on what is socially acceptable.

This seems to be the orthodox Freudian view of sublimation. In this, we have a store of original psychic energy (*libido*) which builds up and seeks satisfaction (or pleasure) in release of tension. Sublimation means directing this energy from the ordinary instinctual channels, which for various reasons may not be open to it, into other forms of activity which may be socially acceptable and in accordance with one's own sense of the reality principle. This is a picture of a fund of energy which can be redirected without changing its nature. In *Civilization and its Discontents* Freud saw this kind of sublimation both as essential for civilised life and yet also as continually frustrating the individual—a pessimistic picture; but even if the prospects for sublimation on this view of energy were less pessimistic, we could still ask whether it is the right one.

The question is whether the energy itself remains unchanged, or whether the kind of satisfaction sought and maybe found can affect its character. It is difficult to see how it could, if we just talk about 'energy' in this connection. But this may not be the right word, since so-called psychic energy is not like physical energy a term for measurable work done. Let us start another way, and speak of *desires* and the kind of things towards which they are directed. If it is a fact that there is just desire, it might be switched from one kind of object to another without being modified.

But the question is not only how to get satisfaction—even more satisfaction—through things of superior quality. It is whether the desire itself may acquire a different character according to the things towards which it is directed—'Where your treasure is, there will your heart be also.' 'Treasure in heaven' may stand not for the location of what one wants but for a reorientation which can change the character of one's desires. If, instead of thinking of the psyche as a store of energy which can be sent through different pipes, we think of it as a system of active ways of responding and relating, both to one's internal states and to external objects, then a desire to read or write poetry may be not only a different desire, but a different kind of desire from the desire to play pushpin. It was the Utilitarians' way of speaking of pleasure as though it were a thing in itself apart from what it was *pleasure in* that made them think otherwise. There may be an internal relation between a desire and what may be called its intentional object. 'To play pushpin' is an intentional object (as distinguished from the object as a piece of hardware in the external world, in this case the pushpin apparatus: pushpin, I believe, is a kind of shove ha'penny). A desire is not an atomic event; it is a way in which a person is feeling in relation to something. So the desire is characterised by being the desire for x, and by the different sides of a person's nature it brings into play. This might be said to be a linguistic question of how one describes desires. But it may also be an empirical question. The actual desire itself may have a different quality according to how it is oriented and to what, and this may also affect the other parts of the person's psyche. This may be a question for psychologists, and a controversial one, but I do not subscribe to the view that philosophers ought not to raise empirical questions, especially in a case where I think many psychologists proceed on the hedonistic assumption, that there are just desires and their satisfactions. So our question is whether a person can come not only to change the things he desires, but whether he himself also is changed through changing the thing he desires, in more than the trivial sense in which A-desiring-x is different from A-desiring-y. And, most crucially, can he change from a person who desires things because he can use them for his own purposes to being a person who has come to appreciate things and adapt himself to his appreciation?

It is in these terms that I should want to see the distinction between 'objectivity' and 'subjectivity' in judgements where values as well as facts are involved. It is the distinction between what one happens to want and what one can come to appreciate—a change in orientation towards learning to appreciate, an orientation guided by the conviction that there is indeed something to be learnt, and that this includes ways of living, the life-styles to which we commit ourselves.

One might say that what is learnt is how better to follow one's chosen life-style, 'better' and 'worse' having an application within this context. Then if one's life-style is egoistic, promoting one's

own interests and manipulating other people to serve one's purposes, one can learn to do this more skilfully and come to appreciate subtler methods. What of saying that there might be a better
life-style? Here one must perforce make a first-person recommendation, hoping nevertheless that there are considerations by
which it can be supported. I shall here only indicate some features
in what might be such a life-style. I should put high any life-style
which accepts the complexity of moral issues; the need to think
about the worthiness of one's projects; the mutuality of relationships with other people; the need for courage in one's civic roles as
well as generosity in one's more personal face-to-face dealings. I
should also rank highly the capacity to see how proposed actions
could threaten rather than strengthen mutual trust, since I see
this trust as a condition for most of the enterprises and relationships which we find rewarding. All this will call on one to enlarge
one's imagination in seeing the situations in which one acts; not
only seeing single chains of cause and effect, but ramifications and
repercussions. It will mean trying to see what one's proposed
actions will be likely to do to other people, not only in external
help or hurt, but in their effects on internal feelings. A person who
sees proposed actions in terms of his own interests can simplify the
issues by reducing them to one perspective; he may thereby make
his own task of decision easier, but there will be aspects of the
situation which he has not opened himself to appreciate. I maintain that a way of living in which such considerations are taken
into account is one in which moral judgement is more likely to
grow in capacity to face complex issues. It may be said that the
considerations I have named are mainly factual, concerned with
getting a more adequate grasp of situations. This is so, but I think
that the attempt so to see situations is likely to be value-laden.
Certain values, notably fairness and sympathy, will be congenial
to the effort to detach our view from a weighting in favour of our
own interests. Even if not natural features of situations fairness
and sympathy can be, to use a medieval term, 'connatural' to such
a way of looking at the facts.

One has, I think, to decide to make the venture of believing that
one can come to appreciate situations in greater depth, and this is
a venture reinforced through following it rather than one whose
correctness can be demonstrated at the start. The start is to
change our orientation from preoccupation with our own interests
to liberty of spirit to see things disinterestedly.[18] This is what Iris

Murdoch was saying, and I think she was right. Such growth in appreciation could, however, be aesthetic. In morality we speak of will and action as well as of vision and discernment, where discernment is not only of what is given, but in judging what to do.

Moral judgements are concerned with what one ought to do, and I have connected the force of 'ought' with that of *commitment*. The strictest form is that of a commitment where we have made an undertaking—a promise for instance, or a contract. More generally, it can be where a way of behaving is seen as consequent on a way of life which we have decided to try to follow. Moreover, there may be practices which are at present part of the legal or institutional requirements of our society, and we have accepted them on the whole, though we do not personally approve of some of their particular features. Feeling ourselves consequentially committed to these particular features, especially if they are part of the law, would be a matter of weaker obligation, and sometimes disapproval can be overriding.

Thus commitment may produce the sense of pressure in obligation, but beyond commitment there is still the factor of *judgement*. That I did *x* because I had committed myself to do it may indeed often be sufficient justification, but there are times when it is arguable that the right thing would be to break a particular commitment, and at a deeper level there is the question of breaking off a commitment to a way of life where this is seen to involve purposes and methods of which one can no longer approve. Arthur Koestler in *The God that Failed* has described the crises of conscience of various members of the Communist Party, himself included, who had come to the painful decision that they must make the break. W. W. Bartley, in *The Retreat to Commitment* (London, 1964) has effectively castigated the view that the fact of commitment renders one immune from self-criticism, and from reconsideration of one's position.

We are therefore brought back again to the need for *judgement*. Moral judgement is about what one ought to do in the particular case, and though the *pressure* in an 'ought' may be traced to commitments, judgement is not bound by the past, but seeks to assign priorities in the present. This is where *conscience* may be seen as a union of intellectual discrimination with moral responsibility. Conscience is generally looked on as facing backwards—the inbuilt super-ego which produces guilt feelings over the infringement of an already implanted code. Kant, although his moral will is a good deal more than the super-ego, uses forensic metaphors of a court of conscience which condemns or acquits after the deed. But can there also be a forward-looking conscience—perhaps pointed to in St Thomas Aquinas' view of it as an intellectual activity in making moral judgements?[19] Such a conscience could be thought of as an internalised Ideal Observer, commenting on (sometimes laughing at) one's judgements and behaviour. Sometimes it may not function as a self-awareness separate from the actual activity of judging; the Ideal Observer's qualities may have been so internalised as to function as a present guide in judging. Such a conscience would not only produce a sense of guilt when one's existing principles were not being observed. It could be a first-hand power of judgement which might originate new principles. Religious views which have connected conscience with 'the voice of God' have, I think, usually been concerned with the possibility of non-obvious and difficult moral decisions, rather than with failures to observe an implanted moral code. Those religious views which sever the link between the notion of 'the Will of God' and the notion of conscience, and produce an amoral notion of the Will of God, do not allow for the development of this kind of conscience, which may not indeed give infallible guidance, but which can be a growing point in moral judgement. It is adequately represented neither in the Existentialist's conception of 'authenticity', nor in the appeal to spontaneous judgement favoured by the upholders of 'situation ethics'. These want the fruits of a developed moral and intellectual capacity without regard to what may be necessary for its cultivation.

Moral judgement does not take the place of other kinds of judgement—practical, technical, aesthetic, intellectual. There are many matters of such judgements, as also 'play' activities—which are not matters of morality in their own internal rationale. But moral questions may come up over how and when they should be pursued. The point was put by J. M. Brown, now lecturer in the New University of Ulster in Coleraine, when he was a pupil of mine in Manchester. In an essay on 'Can we take moral holidays?' he said, 'We are not always [actively] on duty, but we are always on call.' Considerations affecting other people, or our own integrity, may obtrude themselves while we are doing something in which it had seemed no moral problems were involved. Morality can be pervasive in the sense that moral questions can come up both over the consequences of what we are doing, and over the manner in which it is done. And then there may be the question whether this is what we ought to be doing *now*.

'What I ought to be doing now' is surely not just being moral. Morality is not so much an activity in itself as on the back of other activities, concerned with what one does in them, and how and when. The particular feature in morality dominant at any given time will be likely to be that most characteristically associated with whatever activity we are involved in. In acting politically, the feature of purpose will be dominant, in acting in a legal or administrative capacity the emphasis will be on principles to be applied impartially. But other factors within morality may become relevant both to the occasion and manner of what is done; there are times when a purpose in politics may be challenged for a principle, and times when sympathetic discretion will temper judicial impartiality, and times in personal relations when keen-edged criticism is more appropriate than tolerant acceptance. To judge morally calls for one to be alert to this complexity; to see that no activity can rightly be carried on by maintaining a form that can become a stereotype, still less by going by the book. There is also the complexity of what constitutes a 'situation'. The facts of situations in which one has to act and the likely consequences of one's actions are not just single events leading to other events in a single track; they are networks proliferating into other networks. Moreover, one may judge an action to be right because it fits a new emerging state of affairs, not just the alignment of the situation as it now is. One can never see more than a part of this complexity, but one can try to remove the blinkers which confine one's view.

I have said that I see the most appropriate moral stance as a B-type teleology in which one cultivates liberty of spirit in order the better to make moral judgements, in order the better to pursue whatever purposes one thinks worth pursuing, and to know better how to act in one's dealings with other people (the three-tier teleology here may sound complicated, but it is introduced deliberately, in order to bring out the difference from an A-type teleology which is set on one immediate purpose). Liberty of spirit is not itself a goal to be sought (like 'liberation' in some religious teachings) so much as a disposition to be cultivated in pursuing one's goals; it is to get away from one's preconceptions and from being emotionally preoccupied by chagrin, disappointment, envy, fear, so that one may act with something approaching what Kant called the good will, and with more clarity as to the issues involved. Such a B-type teleology calls for a moral psychology defining the condition of mind in which it can be pursued. I prefer to speak of 'liberty of spirit' rather than 'disinterestedness', since, though both are terms for detachment, the latter suggests detachment from giving preferential treatment to one's own interests, while the former, more widely and positively, suggests being released from emotional self-preoccupation so as to make one's judgements with greater clarity. The clarity may be in seeing what effort is required to carry out some purpose or purposes—as we say, counting the cost. Or it may be in seeing the effects on other people of what we are doing, their feelings, needs and interests. Neither of these aspects can, I believe, be omitted from morality, nor will their demands always point in the same direction or be mutually supporting, nor is there any overall principle by which these conflicts can be resolved. Liberty of spirit may help one to live with this moral complexity without succumbing in confusion and indecision.

When an 'ought' is purely deliberative, it is a question of what act would best solve a practical problem, without connecting it with wider issues such as one's background commitment to a way of living, to longer-term purposes one thinks it right to pursue, and to how one thinks one should conduct one's dealings with other people. When it is so connected, then the 'ought' will be seen as putting a moral and not only a practical problem. People will weigh what they see as moral considerations differently, their dominant emphasis giving a final moral reason for their decision. This is not to say that if a problem is seen as having moral implications, these will always be taken as final. Of course people can choose to disregard morality; what I have been concerned to question is not that one can disregard morality, but various high-minded reasons which are sometimes given for doing so. Nor does a decision in terms of a particular moral emphasis absolve one from conflict, from asking 'what ought I to do?' where each of the possible but incompatible actions may be seen as presenting a moral claim. I should prefer to see such cases not as conflicting 'oughts', but as conflicting obligations, where obligations (in the plural) are claims generally in virtue of commitments, but need not always be morally final considerations. I prefer to speak of conflicts of obligations here rather than, with W. D. Ross, of *prima facie* duties.[20] When one decides for one of the incompatibles, this is not to deny that there was moral force in the rejected alternative. It may well be what we call a choice of evils; there are problems for which there is no satisfactory solution, no possible action without a debit side, nor one which can be done without pain and without regret.

In some conflicts, one may judge that the pull, for instance, of some important piece of work, should take precedence over the claim on one of another person. One may of course say 'To Hell with morality; this is what I intend to do'; then one is deliberately deciding to be amoral. The person who sees the conflict as a moral dilemma may come up with the same answer in practice as the amoral decider. He differs not in his answer, but in having struggled with it as a moral problem, and this is not just a trivial difference; it is through such struggles that the power of moral judgement may grow. He may also feel called on to make such restitution as he can to the person whose claim has been over-ridden.[21]

The full stringency of morality is realised when one sees both that one's judgement is problematic and that one must take responsibility for it. It may indeed be that morality can only be final if it is allowed to be problematic, not given in absolute principles. The transcendental reference in the sovereignty of Good can put a question-mark against the finality of any purpose, however imperious, and the universal applicability of any prin-ciple, however imperative. The person who sees the claims of some achievement as putting him 'beyond good and evil' may be right in so far as he interprets these as the customs of some particu-lar social morality. But if he cannot look towards a good beyond his 'beyond good and evil', he forfeits a corrective against what may also become a blinkered vision. His purpose may be a noble one: to paint a great picture, or to liberate his country. But the moment may come when something else—perhaps something vitally affecting another person—may need to take precedence. Or perhaps it need not; but under the sovereignty of Good the possibility is not foreclosed.

13 Metaphysical Postscript

> The intellect of man is forced to choose
> Perfection of the life or of the work.

Yeats says in 'The Choice', pointing to a dilemma. We have been tempted to say that concentration on an achievement, however high, if it overrides morality in personal relations may in the end corrupt its own practice, ruthlessness infecting dedication. This may not necessarily happen. What can be said is that human relations are an inescapable part of life; even if to disregard the feelings and interests of others may not corrupt a person's main work, it may blunt his sensibilities.

In any case, I have said that this is a conflict within morality itself. There is, I believe, no satisfactory meta-ethical view which can harmonise the claims of social morality and individual aim under a unifying principle. When these conflicts arise, the mediating factor is not an abstract principle but moral judgement, fallible yet capable of development, one condition of development being readiness to face this very complexity.

The conflicts are there, and they can be exacerbated by the fact that the pursuit of a dominant aim and the imperiousness of duty can both acquire metaphysical overtones. We saw that terms like 'calling', and indeed 'destiny', can underpin the single-minded pursuit of an end. An absolute quality can also be attached to the notion of duty, though this is more likely to take the form of a categorical imperative in an autonomous morality than a religious or metaphysical demand. Morality may be seen as an 'ultimate concern', and so may the pursuit of an end or a creative venture. The word 'call' can be used of both, suggesting that here is not just a matter of choice. But can there be two 'ultimate concerns'? If there is no way in which they can be shown to coincide, one must yield in ultimacy; or a person may try to keep to both and be split between them.

147

An 'ultimate concern' is not just an overriding concern at any time which could be what one happened to be most concerned about, and this could vary with circumstances. An 'ultimate concern' would be what one finally draws on in one's priorities. As standing for something steady and not just episodic, 'ultimate concern' was an expression put into currency by Paul Tillich, who defined a person's religion as whatever was his ultimate concern. This suggested that there might be people who make a religion out of e.g. football. The use of the word 'religion' for such concerns seems unnatural. A religious concern can be an obsession, but it is also generally something which is thought of as demanding loyalty. So it might be said, does the football club of which one is a supporter. The question is whether one makes it a supreme loyalty; if so it could well be a 'religion' in Tillich's sense.

When 'ultimate concern' is given metaphysical overtones, it does not only refer to what may be a dominant drive at any time—or even what, when I sit down in a cool hour, I decide I care about most. It will acquire normative overtones, as something to which I am 'called' or 'destined', or 'meant to do'. And it might be said that if we could get rid of these metaphysical overtones, then moral decisions about what I ought to do could be made with less emotion and less rhetoric.

But what if the metaphysics are not only overtones? What if there is some actual ground which is more than a matter of our own wills, or even aptitudes and temperaments, why these deep, dedication-producing urges should be followed? Is the daemonic person right who sees their imperiousness as a call to follow a destiny which need not be a moral one, or, if he sees his motivation to follow it as his moral absolute, this is something distinct from and beyond the morality of right and wrong in conduct between persons? This latter may then be seen as conformity to custom or convention. Even this, as we have said, is not to be despised. Conventions can be institutions (in a wide sense of 'institution') devised for social living, and their more and less viable forms can be matters of serious argument. Morality is at least this; but its power to challenge the potential amorality in appeals to 'destiny' will be the stronger if it is more than this.

Here the old Greek distinction of '*Nomos*' (νόμος) and '*Physis*' (φύσις) may be brought into service. *Nomos*, 'Law', is made by convention. Conventions need not be merely arbitrary; there can be reasons for adopting some rather than others, but they are, as contemporary moralists would say, prescriptive. *Physis*, 'Nature', is a matter of how things are, and how they should behave is said to be connected in the last resort with how they are—perhaps, in a still more question-begging way, with 'how they really are'. This has produced the 'Natural Law' theory of morality, which is vulnerable as giving absolute validity to what may be local principles within a particular tradition. It has also underestimated the importance of *Nomos* morality as institutional convention, particularly in the legal sense. 'Natural Law' may be invoked as a means of moral criticism of existing law. It is indeed important to be able to criticise this, but 'Natural Law' conflates the moral criticism with the law itself. (Aristotle dryly advised young lawyers, when they had no case according to the law of the land, to refer to the Law of Nature, and cite the *Antigone* of Sophocles[1]—the notion has its persuasive as well as its critical uses.)

'Natural Justice' is, I believe, on stronger ground. 'Natural' here is used to refer to principles which are neither matters of arbitrary choice, nor of revelation, nor of the fiat of a sovereign power. They are principles of procedure which can be seen to be connected non-contingently with the intention of arriving at fair decisions, though they cannot, of course, ensure them. They are non-contingent in being part of what is meant by the impersonal impartiality, the universalisability, which, if not a sufficient criterion of all moral decisions, has its place in the morality of judicial decision. That no one should be judge in his own case, and that a person should be told what he is accused of so that he can make his defence—these maxims of Natural Justice are principles of procedure which are embedded in our Common Law. I have said that they are part of what is meant by judicial fairness. Besides appealing to reason, the principles of Natural Justice are 'connatural' with fact, as procedures enabling facts to be ascertained with impartiality. They are indeed principles, and not facts, but it can be said that by using them there is in fact more likelihood of arriving at decisions which are both fair and seen to be fair.

Certain principles can be shown to be conducive to certain desired ends, and sometimes also the principles share the quality of the end, and this is so in the case of Natural Justice. To be allowed to make one's defence, either in person or through a lawyer or some other advocate, is not only a means to something fair, but is also itself fair. Sometimes a person may choose to defend himself and do it so clumsily that we say he would have done better to have kept his mouth shut. Nevertheless we may still think that it would have been unfair not to have let him try. Here the deontological aspect of principle, which falls within a teleological setting can become dominant. This is because the teleology is B-type and not A-type; the principles conducive to the end are not only instrumental but also share the quality to be promoted.

What about the ends within which such principles have their setting? The old distinction of natural and conventional morality pegged natural morality to an end which was that of the proper development of human nature, thus basing itself on a metaphysic of morals. There are certainly difficulties in such a moral teleology, not least in setting up a specific goal of human development or fulfilment. 'Chief ends' may be variously envisaged, and can only be commended as goals in the vaguest terms. There may, however, be B-type orientations which persons may seek to cultivate, and which may encourage the growth of moral judgement. I have suggested 'liberty of spirit' as a progressively achievable orientation, which would make for clarity of judgement in deciding what specific ends one should pursue, in seeing what is involved in following them seriously, and in trying to discern what one should do in the human situations in which one finds oneself.

'Liberty of spirit' is akin to, but not I think, identical with the 'liberation' which is sought in some forms of religious training. 'Liberation' needs moral discipline for its cultivation, but may (I think) be valued as an end which can be beyond morality. Liberty of spirit not only needs moral discipline to overcome self-preoccupation, but is itself valued as a means towards the improvement of moral judgement. It is not sought as a state 'beyond good and evil'.

It is significant that the contrast to 'good' here is not 'bad' but 'evil'. What is evil is not just infringing a rule, still less a mistaken action, or one with unfortunate consequences. A bad action can be any of these, as well as being an action of which I disapprove. 'Good' and 'bad', as terms of approbation and disapprobation, express preferences. This need not be all—I spoke in the last chapter of 'good' as expressing appreciation as well as preference—but they are at least this. To call an action evil, is, I think, to say more than that I disapprove of it, even that I strongly disapprove of it. Indeed, if it is used of actions, it is used when they are seen as expressing an inner disposition. An evil disposition is one in which a person has come to enjoy behaviour which hurts others and which leads him to sow mistrust. Hatred, envy, spite, are states of mind which in fact, and not by convention, destroy the conditions of mutual trust and confidence which are the underlying conditions for such mutual enterprises and relationships as people can find continuingly rewarding. Evil is a word describing what we may call a 'spiritual' disposition; a state of consciousness and of the springs of action. If it is not just moral badness, but a corruption of the springs of action in a person's mind, this is why writers like Dostoevsky, who see deeply into these, also see deeply into evil. Evil as a corruption comes from an urge to go deeper than merely customary morality, and even than the rational morality of reciprocity. If we could stay within a purely 'Nomos' type of morality, the potentiality of evil might not arise.

The daemonic person who claims to be beyond good and evil may not in fact have an evil disposition; indeed, his very concentration may give him a certain kind of moral strength. But he is not on his guard against letting his preoccupation with his own project, and the spiritual powers he may have developed in following it, so harden him into self-centredness that his consciousness and springs of action get corrupted, and he becomes incapable of clarity of vision in seeing what he is doing to other people. His orientation may then turn to evil.

To return to the metaphysical overtones. I have said that appeals to deep urges can be put in language about 'calling', 'fate', 'destiny', suggesting that we have to do with more than a matter of our own choice. Some deep urges may feel as though they were more than this, and yet one may come to see them as snares. Ancient Greek writers, especially Homer and the dramatists, looked on a person's non-rational impulses as sometimes being the invasion of his personality by divine powers, so that he could not help doing what he did. This may be inspiration, where Apollo and the Muses took over; more often it is seen as the inrush of a divine power quoted as an excuse, or at least in mitigation. When Agamemnon disclaims having chosen to deprive Achilles of Briseis the fair-cheeked, he says 'Zeus and my fate and the Fury who walks in darkness are the cause; for they put fierce blindness, *ate*, into my mind in the assembly on that day when I deprived Achilles of his prize. . . . But since I was blinded by *ate* and Zeus took away my wits, I am willing to make my peace and give abundant recompense!'[3]

Euripides is instructive here; he begins to psychologise these invasions of passion, provocation, euphoria. 'Kupris, it appears, is no goddess, but something bigger', says the Nurse in the *Hippolytus*, turning from the infatuated Phaedra to the statue of Aphrodite.[4] The Greek dramatists and Homer were struggling with the way in which surges of passion and intense inner conflicts seem both part of ourselves and not ourselves.

In Christianity divine power is called 'grace'; in the words of the Easter collect, 'as by thy special grace preventing us thou dost put into our minds good desires'. Well-meaning ministers, knowing that 'prevent' in ordinary contemporary English means just the opposite of what the collect says, sometimes alter it to 'assisting us'. This fails to grasp the nettle. '*Pre*vent' in its old sense of 'going before' means taking an initiative. But should we not take the smooth with the rough, and accept 'good desires' as well as blind surges of passion as parts of ourselves? There are indeed imperious desires, in sex for instance, or the craving for power. Creative effort, we are told, can draw on these energies; it can also be affected by their self-centredness and this can happen with the powers sought through religion. They can be what the counter-culture calls an 'ego trip'. But can there be a power of 'grace'?

There is no one way of seeing 'the relation of religion and morality' because both are problematic, so that their relation will differ according to how they are being considered. Religion can be a matter of single-minded devotion, but this can be to dark gods; it can be a daemonic and even a fanatical obsession, and in these ways it can be a threat to social morality. Traditional societies have been well aware of the threat, and through their forms of upbringing and their rituals have taken means to channel religion into a support for the values necessary to their communal life. This, is, indeed, the way in which religion is seen by one influential school in social anthropology, and such symbolic moralism may seem to hold of certain simple forms of religious teaching, concerned largely with how we should treat our neighbours. A friend who had to listen to a number of children's sermons in Methodist churches said that the message which came across to him was 'Be kind to Granny and the cat, especially the cat'. Persons with original spiritual gifts (including surely those in the tradition of the early Methodists) may well feel that they must leave such moralism behind.

The great religions, and also the so-called primitive religions, besides having a strong communal bent, are concerned not only with the quest for and the use of inner powers, but with the moral qualities which can inform them. Beyond the enhancement of powers, which can be dark as well as deep, lies 'liberation' from self, the losing of self to find it, the growth of liberty of spirit. The moral conditions for this state are detachment from the passions which enlarge and indulge the possessive self, and the teachings of what in the Christian tradition is called 'ascetic theology' are concerned with their mastery.

In ascetic theology, the 'Seven Deadly Sins' are expressions of a state of mind which deadens or corrupts one's perceptions of spiritual things, including sensitivity in relation to other people. Thus, *Pride* is a 'concupiscence of the mind' in thinking too much or too highly of oneself.[5] *Covetousness* (or avarice) is called by St Paul 'Idolatry'—it is not just wanting material things, but being obsessed by wanting them. Lust is 'a fleshly greed or gluttony, for physical excitement'.[6] *Envy* is a state of mind which can lead people to hate or want to destroy where they cannot possess. *Gluttony* is the excessive eating which can deaden people's awareness of spiritual things. *Anger*, though it may not always in itself be wrong, is a sin when it distorts a man's perspective so that he gets out of control and can contradict himself in what he says and does. *Sloth* is not only physical laziness (though this too), but mental, leading one to refuse to pay attention to disturbing facts, or to make the necessary effort to understand them. The 'Seven Deadly Sins' are deadly because they deaden; they corrupt and can destroy clarity of spiritual perception. They are qualities infecting a person's springs of action, and so affect not only his own 'liberation', but also his dealings with other people

This is one of the meeting points of religion and morality. While religion is not morality, people have always known that it must either become moral or it will destroy morality. White magic is shadowed by black magic; the 'terrible strength of the saints'[7] is matched by the terrible and potentially destructive strength of the daemonic; Lucifer is a fallen angel; Bunyan's Christian saw that there was a way down to Hell from the very gate of Heaven.

These are dramatic expressions; behind them there is a perennial problem: the union of the two 'ultimate concerns'. On the one hand there are the deep urges which make for creativity and the

search for self-fulfilment. On the other hand there are the claims
of morality and the elusive attraction of goodness.

Following Iris Murdoch on 'the Sovereignty of Good' I have
spoken of appreciation of goodness as needing clear and disinterested perception, adding that for morality there should also be
disinterested intention of the will. 'Disinterestedness' may be
impersonal detachment, but it need not be inhuman if the
detachment is not from love of what is prized, but from self-
seeking in its attainment, so that it becomes the more positive
quality of liberty of spirit.

This may be relevant to the notion of 'the Will of God'. The
notion is most characteristically invoked not in day-to-day decisions where one knows tolerably well what to do, but in difficult,
critical decisions, where what to do is highly problematic. In such
cases, a person may find a way of acting which strengthens his
powers of responsible action, and in which he yet seems to be
following more than his own choice. Decisions made in such
contexts can be made gropingly, beyond what a person clearly
sees as right or wrong. Yet they need not be amoral as 'beyond
good and evil'. They may extend our moral notions in non-
obvious ways. They draw on and also release creative power.

Such power comes, I believe, from learning to live from a deep
centre of the mind—the old mystical writers spoke of the *fun-
dus*—and directing the energy thus produced towards a love of
goodness, a love of God—or whatever term for a concept of
transcendental perfection we can use that may provide a corrective to self-centredness and moral complacency. But if expressions
such as 'the Sovereignty of Good' or 'the Will of God' are to have
more than a formal function, correcting self-centredness and
reminding us that our moral judgements are always corrigible,
they will carry metaphysical significance. They are indeed ideals
to which we can aspire; can they also point to efficacious realities?

Religious life, when it is not just social convention or the search
for self-enlargement, moves between the notions of creative power
and of some sovereign good. Traditional theism has held that
these are united in a single source. To think of this source as a God
who is 'a moral Being', or 'moral Lawgiver', seems to me to
underestimate the extent to which morality and law are human
institutions. Moreover, the imperious creative urges which make
people want to talk in terms of 'call' or 'destiny' can have a
non-moral character, which gives force to metaphysics of creative

power beyond good and evil. Nevertheless, I see religions as too intimately concerned with morality to be happy about leaving creative power on the one side, and morality as a matter of purely prescriptive contrivance on the other, to divide the field between them.

I come back to the contrast of '*Physis*' and '*Nomos*'. To end with a contrast between 'Nature' as a source of amoral energy and a conventionally constructed morality, which is a device for how people may live together, fits 'the autonomy of ethics', and puts the responsibility for it squarely on ourselves. It would be a matter of rules and recommendations, free from any religious sanction, except in so far as religion is seen as symbolising moral values and fostering moral cohesion within a social group. Such a view says a word about religion and morality which should not be ignored, but it need not be the last word. Indeed, even social morality draws on inner resources, such as the spirit of generosity, which make it viable. I see the distinction of 'Nature' and 'Convention' in morality not as the assertion of a universal metaphysically grounded code versus local conventionally constructed codes, but as pointing to the dependence of even conventional morality on the development of resources within the person, which can be trained and fostered by imaginative effort, but not just set up by deliberate choice.[8] This is not a matter of the sanctioning of a particular code, but of an orientation of the springs of action. One orientation is disinterestedness, consistency in applying principles to oneself as well as to others, and impartial regard for interests. I have spoken of 'liberty of spirit', rather than disinterestedness, as I see this as a more positive orientation in which one can get free of one's self-preoccupations, fears and defences, so that some of the hindrances to wise judgement can be overcome. Seen in relation to morality, it might be called an instrumental orientation, since it would be an attitude of mind in which moral judgements were made. It would also be an attitude of mind towards the matters about which judgements are made, freeing one for instance, from personal obsession with any one of them, and in this too it could be an aid to moral judgement. For I see morality, not as a thing in itself, but as a way of thinking about and disposing our actions over what projects we should pursue; how and when to pursue them; how we should conduct our dealings with other people; and how we should become aware of and educate the basic feelings which enter into our approvals and disapprovals. Liberty of spirit would be an orientation towards the morality of achievements, as well as towards the morality of interpersonal relations, and it could enable us to accept that there are occasions when the different aspects of morality call on us to reorder our priorities.

I have said that I see no overall view which will allow us to circumvent conflicts between different aspects, and that we should accept that morality has this complexity. Liberty of spirit does not allow us to escape conflicts, but can bring simplification into our attitude in the face of them. This can call for a reorientation in our desires, as well as a capacity to detach ourselves from them. Some religious teachers speak of the 'transformation' of the self, and exercises are recommended for the 'transformation of consciousness'. 'Transformation' means change, and all changes are not necessarily for the better.[9] We can be concerned not just with transformation, but with such changes in desires, motives, aspirations, as will encourage growth in ability to discern the issues for moral judgement, and in the power to make it.

I come back to what I said in the last chapter about there being an internal relation between a desire and that to which it is directed, so that the desire for x can be a different kind of desire from the desire for y, rather than there being a charge of appetitive feeling directed to one object or to another. There are indeed basic physical needs where the desire to satisfy or relieve them can hardly be changed, though we can learn to deal with them in socially acceptable ways (the toilet training of children is an obvious example). The desire for food is perhaps unalterable as physical hunger, though in fortunate circumstances we can desire not just to satisfy it as hunger, but to satisfy it in conjunction with the conviviality of a meal enjoyed with others and controlled by good manners and mutual consideration. What we would do under circumstances of gnawing starvation is another matter. The late Leonard Wilson told me that when he was imprisoned by the Japanese as Bishop of Singapore, and it came to handing plates of food, he could bring himself to offer them to his companion hoping that the latter might take the smaller helping, though he could not bring himself deliberately to hand him the larger one. But he knew a man in the prison who could do just that. Liberty of spirit towards desires is thus not always a matter of eradicating them, which may be impossible, but of rising above self-preoccupation with satisfying them, and this freedom can come through an orientation towards the love of goodness, the love of God, the love of one's fellow men—whatever expression one can use here—which can come to dominate the deepest layers of the personality.

The daemonic person can be living from a deep level of desire directed towards an ideal, and he may be right to see this as more than a matter of his personal choice and personal satisfaction. But he has not won the liberty of spirit towards himself which could prevent him from ruthless use of others as means to his ideal. He has the strength which comes from one kind of moral simplification, that of setting oneself an overriding purpose, and disregarding the complicating factor of concern for the needs and interests of other people. For there are indeed these different and often discordant features in morality, and I have said that an adequate view must start from this complexity. The daemonic man's assertion of purpose is morally blinkered, as is also in another way the deontological morality of rigorous principles. Yet there may be a simplification which can enable us to live with this complexity, and this comes not from escaping conflicts, but by cultivating liberty of spirit in moral judgement. This includes readiness to *think*, so as to see the facts of situations and their likely consequences in their multiple relations. It is not just a matter of intuitive response that can short-circuit thinking. It calls for the growth of an 'unconfined generosity' which can so permeate the springs of action that it releases moral power. The condition for this is spoken of in religious literature in phrases such as 'losing one's life to find it', 'self-abandonment'; it is more likely to be a matter of learning a continual process than a dramatic episode. There may be other ways of describing this condition, not put in recognisably religious language, yet pointing to a re-orientation of the self that releases powers of moral judgement and moral courage.

People always ask the question whether such liberating power is 'part of our own minds' or 'comes from outside ourselves'. Put as an antithesis I find this unanswerable. If it is part of ourselves, it comes from a reorientation of the springs of action which can overcome what in religious language was called 'the natural self'. William James spoke of continuity with 'a wider self through which saving experiences come'.[10] If this wider self is the unconscious mind, it is very unlike current psycho-analytic pictures of this. It may also be thought of as the creative power of the world, canalised in an individual who no longer only draws on it for his purposes, but lets it work through him as a liberating power turned towards good. This is not a 'moral law' but a deep source of moral steadiness, deeper, I believe, than that on which the daemonic person draws, and it feeds love and wisdom in moral judgement. A power to hold together creative effort and outgoing love will not free us from conflicts between the claims of some projected achievement and the claims of other people. But it will prevent us from turning the former into a reason for ruthlessness and the latter into a reason for moralism, and it can make us able to live with moral complexity. There is a way of fulfilment here which people have sought, and some have succeeded in finding, and which can well be missed. In this the old 'Law of Nature' moralists were right, though they were not right in trying to codify conditions for this way in a set of rules, rather than looking for them in the resources on which moral judgement can draw.

To return to my original image of the prism. It was but an image, pointing to a complexity in our moral vision. The unseen white light can pass through the prism, but the complex of colours remains; we may fasten selectively on one at any given time, yet we see it as but one colour in the spectrum. It does not eclipse the others, and if we are fortunate it can even enhance them.

Notes

CHAPTER 1

1. *Phaedo* 99d. 'Second line of approach' is R. Bluck's translation in his edition.
2. *Republic* 352d.
3. 'Situation ethics' is the name of a view held by some contemporary Christian moralists that right actions are judged through applying a spirit of love and spontaneity in individual situations, and not by following principles. It is thus an instance of concentrating on one single feature in the spectrum.
4. I shall be looking at this in Chapter 9; I suggest it may be a kind of moral Narcissism.
5. *The Limits of Purpose* (O.U.P., 1932), p. 79.
6. 'Essentially Contested Concepts', *Proceedings of the Aristotelian Society*, 1956. See also his book, *Philosophy and the Historical Understanding* (New York, 1964), chapters VIII and IX. Alasdair MacIntyre in 'The Essential Contestability of Social Concepts' (*Ethics*, vol. 84, no. 1), uses the notion in speaking of how some (not all) social concepts have no fixed criteria for their application over periods of time. He instances 'political party'. Steven Lukes in 'Relativism; Cognitive and Moral' (*Aristotelian Society*, Supp. Vol. XLVIII, 1974) also uses the notion in questioning whether there are any indisputable criteria of what counts in moral judgements, since it is possible to cite historical and ethnographic evidence of putative moral systems which violate each of them. These two authors are concerned with shifts of meaning of a concept in different historical and sociological contexts. This does not seem to me as interesting as shifts in emphasis made by different people in the same society and the same period, and even by oneself in different contexts.
7 This feature of moral theories has been brought out by A. Gewirth in 'Meta-Ethics and Normative Ethics', *Mind*, LXIX (April 1960).
8. It is sometimes said that 'ethics' should be the word for theory and 'morality' that for substantive conduct and its principles. I do not think this distinction is systematically observed, and as, in any case, I do not think that the distinction between a theory and normative recommendations can always be sharply drawn, I do not intend to observe it. I shall usually speak of 'morality', but in some contexts I shall speak of 'ethics' where this seems more natural or is the usage of the people I may be discussing. In particular, of course, it is the usage in speaking of 'meta-ethics'.
9. Cambridge, Mass., 1957.

CHAPTER 2

1. The title of a book by H. D. Lasswell, first published in 1936, but, I think, more influential after its republication in 1951. Cf. also *The Language of Politics*, Lasswell *et al.* (Cambridge, Mass., 1949; reprinted, Massachusetts Institute of Technology, 1965), p. 8: 'When we speak of the science of politics, we mean the science of power. Power is decision-making. A decision is a sanctioned choice, a choice which brings severe deprivations to bear against anyone who flouts it.'
2. *Thoughts on the Cause of the Present Discontents*, p. 23, edition of 1770; New Universal Library edition, p. 21.
3. Cf. F. Fanon, *The Wretched of the Earth* (Penguin Books, 1967), esp. p. 74. Sorel also talks like this in *Réflexions sur la violence*.
4. *Power and Personality* (New York, 1948), p. 38.
5. Ibid., p. 160.
6. Cf. ibid., p. 223: 'The political man is one who demands the maximization of his power in relation to all his values, who expects power to determine power, and who identifies with others as a means of enhancing power, position and potential.'
7. *The Second World War*, vol. II, p. 14 (London, 1949).
8. *John Knox*, (London, 1937), p. 116.
9. See his well-known inaugural lecture, *'Political Education'* republished in *Rationalism in Politics* (London, 1962), and the more sustained statement in *On Human Conduct* (Oxford, 1975).
10. *Moral Man and Immoral Society* (New York, 1932 and London, 1933), p. 4.
11. *The Interpretation of Christian Ethics* (New York, 1935), pp.60–1. A still later book, *The Self and the Dramas of History* (1956) is a fuller treatment of the same themes, especially with regard to the complexity of motives in political actions.
12. New York, 1965; Penguin Books, 1968.
13. *Temporal and Eternal* by Charles Péguy, trans. A. Dru (London, 1958), p. 85.

CHAPTER 3

1. I look at some of these in Chapter 10, 'Single-mindedness'.
2. I have given my criticism of it in my *Rules, Roles and Relations* (London, 1966) Chapter VI, 'Sociological Explanation and Individual Responsibility'. Broadly, this is that a sociological analysis can show how people's position in social groups can supply them not only with customary habits, but with motives inclining them to behave in one way rather than another. But this is not a sufficient condition to explain behaviour—you may still choose to wear your rue with a difference.
3. For a discussion of this, see below, pp. 126ff.

CHAPTER 4

1. A selection from this is translated by Nokuro Kobayashi in *The Sketch Book of the Lady Sei Shōnagon* (Wisdom of the East Series, London, 1930).

2. *The Illuminations*, XI, trans. Enid Rhodes Peschel (London, 1973).

3. Ibid., XLII.

4. *A Season in Hell* (trans. Enid Rhodes Peschel), p. 103.

5. *The World as Will and Idea*, Book IV, § 67, p. 484 (English translation by Haldane and Kemp, London, 1883).

6. *Agape and Eros*, Part I, translated by A. G. Hebert (London, 1932); Part II, translated by P. S. Watson (London, 1939). The original appeared in Sweden in 1930. Nygren does not mention that Schopenhauer had drawn the distinction, nor indeed do the two interpretations coincide. Schopenhauer would not, I think, say as Nygren does that *Agape* is 'uncaused' love (in Part II this is rendered 'unmotivated'). The distinction is between *eros* as love for something that fulfils a need in the self and *agape* as selfless love.

7. *The Works of Love*, trans. D. Swenson (O.U.P.), p. 263.

8. *The World as Will and Idea*, Book IV, § 67, p. 484 (English translation by one given me in a letter by Professor Peter Stern, who said that when Schopenhauer uses Christian terminology, as in this phrase, he believes that it is a matter of inadvertent and unacknowledged, often defiant, dependence on that teaching.

9. *The Ironic German* (London, 1958), p. 51.

10. *The Gay Science*, § 107; translation taken from *A Nietzsche Reader*, ed. R. J. Hollingdale (Penguin Classics, 1977). For some further discussion of Nietzsche's metaphysic of morals see below, Chapter 11.

11. *Life with Picasso*, by Françoise Gilot and Carlton Lake (New York, 1964), p. 94. I shall be returning to the argument over this between Picasso and Françoise Gilot when I come to consider the ethics of single-minded commitment. See below, Chapter 10.

12. *The Will to Power*, trans. Walter Kaufmann (London, 1967) § 1067. For Nietzsche this aesthetic acceptance should be a joyful acceptance but, he knows that the world always contains the threat of death and destruction, only overcome in the 'eternal recurrence'. So ecstatic innocence is shadowed by 'the spirit of gravity'. (This is a theme in Peter Stern's study of Nietzsche in the Fontana Modern Masters Series, 1978.)

CHAPTER 5

1. Parts of this chapter are adapted, with permission, from an article of mine, 'Religion and the Social Anthropology of Religion II' in *Theoria to Theory*, vol. III (1968).

2. *The Structure of Social Action* (New York, 1937) p. 391.

3. An expanded version with the same title was published by the Oxford University Press in 1965.

4. Oxford University Press, 1963.

5. See the *Report of the Royal Commission on Capital Punishment* (H.M.S.O., 1953).

6. *The Dynamics of Clanship among the Tallensi* (London, 1945) p. 98.

7. Op. cit., vol. I (Neuchatel, 1912) pp. 161—2.

8. See his *The Forest of Symbols* (Cornell University Press, 1967) esp. pp. 366ff.

9. Republished in *Closed Systems and Open Minds*, ed. M. Gluckman (Edinburgh, 1964).
10. Paris, 1932; English Translation by R. A. Andra and L. Brereton, *The Two Sources of Morality and Religion* (London, 1935).
11. See Steven Lukes, *Emile Durkheim, his Life and Work* (London, 1973) p. 44.
12. For a discussion of this, see Chapter 7.

CHAPTER 6

1. See for instance *The Concept of Prayer* (London, 1965) and 'Religious Beliefs and Language Games' in *The Philosophy of Religion*, ed. B. Mitchell (Oxford, 1971).
2. In *Faith, Hope and Charity in Primitive Religion*, Chapter I, Marett speaks of the 'dynamical mood' as the base of religion. 'To the God-intoxicated man it may seem that henceforth in his omnipotence he can do nothing wrong' (p. 15).
3. *The World of Primitive Man* (New York, 1953) p. 47.
4. Söderblom in *The Living God* (London, 1933) *passim*, but especially Chapter I, starts his account of religion from the notion of power obtained through forms of *askesis*, and he makes a distinction between the 'Yoga' forms which emphasise methods, and the 'Bhakti' forms which emphasise devotion. (This seems to be the source of this distinction, which is used by Professor Ninian Smart: see his article 'What is Comparative Religion?' in *Theoria to Theory*, I, ii (1967), and *Yogi and Devotee* (London, 1968).)
5. Cf. Patanjali, *Yoga Sutras*, Book 3.37 (Harvard Oriental Series, Cambridge, Mass., 1927) p. 266, where it is said that a yogin whose mind is concentrated must avoid those supernormal powers (*siddhis*) even when they come near to him: 'One who looks for the final goal of life, the assuagement of the threefold anguish, how could he have any affection for those supernormal powers which go counter to the attainment of that goal.' And *Dialogues of the Buddha*, Part I (London, 1956) (*Kevaddha Sutta*) describes the supernormal powers with the refrain, 'It is because I perceive the danger in the practice of mystic wonders that I loathe, and abhor, and am ashamed thereof', and he praises the wonder of education. (I owe these references to Freda Wint.)
6. *The Zen Way* (Sheldon Press, London, 1977) p. 83.
7. Margaret Masterman refers to Govinda's prism image in her article 'Integrity in the Religious Quest', Part II (*The Modern Churchman*, vol. XXI, forthcoming). For her the white light shines through the prism and symbolises the redemptive compassionate wisdom of the 'Logos' (Buddhist as well as Christian). She compares the Five Wisdoms with the Christian Five Gifts of the Spirit. This is a mystical prism, pointing to differentiations of an ultimate compassionate wisdom; it goes beyond my prism, which points to a range of different considerations between which our moral judgement may be split. I should like, however, to think that the compassionate wisdom of which she writes is indeed a mystical root of moral judgement, and I shall try to say more about this in my last chapter.
8. *The Teachings of Don Juan* (University of California, 1968, and Penguin

Books, 1970); *A Separate Reality* (1974); *Journey to Ixtlan* (1975); *Tales of Power* (1975); *The Second Ring of Power* (New York and London, 1977).
9. pp. 83—7 (Penguin edition).

CHAPTER 7

1. Etymology: Plato in *Cratylus* 398b suggests δαημων, a perceiver. The New Liddell and Scott prefers a connection with δάιω, 'I apportion' or 'assign'.
2. 'Numen inest: Animism in Greek and Roman Religion', *Harvard Theological Review*, XXVIII (1935).
3. *The Greeks and the Irrational*, p. 23, n. 65 (University of California, 1951).
4. *Works* (ed. Bowring) X, p. 27.
5. R. B. Onians, *The Origins of European Thought about the Body, the Mind, The Soul, the World, Time and Fate* (Cambridge, 1951), says: 'The *genius* was, I suggest, in origin the Roman analogy to the ψυχή as here explained, the life-spirit active in procreation, dissociated from and external to the conscious self that is central in the chest (p. 129). . . . Not only was his genius thus apparently liable to intervene or take possession of a man but we shall see reason to believe that it was, in the time of Plautus, thought to enjoy knowledge beyond what was enjoyed by the conscious self and to give the latter warning of impending events . . . (p. 160). The idea of the *genius* seems to have served in great part as does the twentieth-century concept of an "unconscious mind" influencing a man's life and actions apart from and despite his conscious mind' (p. 161).
6. Goethe's *Autobiography* (*Dichtung und Wahrheit*) trans. John Oxenford, vol. II (1971) pp. 423, 425. Quoted by permission of the publishers, Sidgwick & Jackson.
7. *The Disinherited Mind*, 4th ed. (London, 1975), p. 61.
8. Ibid., pp. 67—8.
9. London, 1970.
10. For some discussion of the notion of the 'Will to Power' and its connection with creative effort, see pp. 95ff.
11. 'A Psychological View of Conscience', *Collected Works* (London, 1964), pp. 437—55.
12. The notion of guardian spirits, not necessarily moral, is widespread in Africa. The official religious leaders will seek to direct people to find a spirit guide who will strengthen them in their role in the community. But the deviants (some are creative originals and some are social menaces) will have their own particular spirit guides (personal communication from Robin Horton). Among the Yoruba of West Nigeria there is the *ori*, which is both a guardian spirit representing one's destiny, and also sometimes spoken of as a deep part of the psyche which guides one. It is not an *orisha* (a deity), but it is the link between a person and the communal *orisha*. It guides his vocation within the community.
13. Heidegger contrasts the voice of *Das Man* (we might say the faceless crowd) with authentic conscience, which, he says, must always be a bad conscience, because it carries guilt feelings produced by going against

communal morality in a call to personal integrity which one can never really achieve. See the discussion of Conscience in *Sein und Zeit*, Part II, Chapter ii (Halle, 1935).

CHAPTER 8

1. Parts of this chapter are adapted from an article of mine 'On "Doing what is right" and "Doing the Will of God" ', which appeared in *Religious Studies*, vol. III, nos. 1 and 2 (1968). I am not concerned in this chapter with the metaphysics of theism, but with the moral bearings in the notion of 'the Will of God'. These passages are used with permission of the publishers, Cambridge University Press.
2. Quoted from the Clarke papers by A. D. Lindsay, in *The Essentials of Democracy* (Oxford, 1930), p. 18 (cf. below, p. 100).
3. Lucretius' comment on the story—'*Tantum religio potuit suadere malorum*'—owes its power to the fact that religious emotions can strengthen and help perpetuate such practices.
4. *Judaism despite Christianity: Letters between Eugen Rosenstock-Huessy and Franz Rosenzweig* (University of Alabama Press, 1969), Letter 15, p. 133 (my translation). The originals formed an Appendix to F.R.'s *Briefe* (Berlin: Schocken-Verlag, 1935).
5. I shall be looking at the notion of conscience in Chapter 12.

CHAPTER 9

1. *Thus Spake Zarathustra*, III §2, 'Of Old and New Law Tables': translation by R. J. Hollingdale in *A Nietzsche Reader* (Penguin, 1977).
2. *Identity: Youth and Crisis* (London, 1968) pp. 22ff. Erikson's view is discussed by W. J. M. Mackenzie in *Political Identity* (Pelican, 1978). Mackenzie is particularly concerned with what it can mean when this notion is extended to groups in a political context.
3. 'L'Homme Nu', in *Mythologiques*, vol. IV (Paris, 1971) p. 572. I owe the reference to Timothy Moore, who also made the translation.
4. *Existentialist Ethics* (Macmillan, 1967) p. 38.
5. In the Putney Debate of 25 October 1647, recorded in the Clarke Papers, ed. A. S. P. Woodhouse, *Puritanism and Liberty* (London, 1938) p. 34.
6. I shall be looking at this aspect of morality in Chapter 11.
7. The prefix 'moral' should be taken to indicate that this is not meant to be simply an empirical psychology. It is a philosophical psychology which Existentialists sometimes indeed call 'ontological'. It can however affect how one sees human psychology, and in psychologists like Carl Rogers it has given rise to a particular Existentialist form of psycho-analysis.
8. When Sartre in *Existentialism and Humanism* (London, 1948) says that in choosing for myself I choose for humanity, he uses Kantian language, but I do not believe that he means that I will the maxim of my action to be a universal law. This would make me impersonal in my choice. Sartre may mean that I am caring about freedom of choice for everyone.

CHAPTER 10

1. Translated from the Danish by Douglas V. Steere (Harper, New York, 1948).

2. In *The Concept of Dread*, translated by Walter Lowrie (O.U.P., 1944) p. 99n.
3. *Ethics and Language* (New Haven, 1944).
4. See Chapter 12.
5. William Faulkner puts it in a letter to a young writer: 'You've got to worry: that's part of it: the suffering and the working, most of all the working, the being willing and ready to sacrifice everything for it—happiness, peace, money, duty too if you are so unlucky.' *Selected letters of William Faulkner*, ed. Joseph Blutner (London, 1977) pp. 295—6.
6. *Life with Picasso* by Françoise Gilot and Carlton Lake, pp. 94—5; copyright © 1964 by McGraw-Hill Inc. New York, and Laurence Pollinger Ltd, London, and used with permission of McGraw-Hill Book Company and Laurence Pollinger Ltd.
7. Ibid., pp. 332—3.
8. There may also be a single-minded, but blinkered vision in a particular approach to social morality: Bentham would be an example of this. And, as John Stuart Mill said of him, 'For our own part we have a large tolerance for one-eyed men, provided their one eye is a penetrating one; if they saw more, they probably would not see so keenly, nor so eagerly pursue one course of enquiry.' But he goes on to say that these one-eyed half-thinkers need to be followed by more complete thinkers. (Essay on Bentham in *Dissertations and Discussions*, Vol. I, reprinted by F. R. Leavis in *Mill on Bentham and Coleridge* (London, 1950) p. 65ff.)
9. See, for instance, David McClelland, *The Achieving Society* (Princeton, 1968). This book argues that self-interest is not the only motive in promoting economic growth, but there is a tendency in some of the literature on N-Ach to talk as though it were a concern for self-advancement. This would be to oversimplify its significance, and not be fair to McClelland.

CHAPTER 11

1. Parts of this Chapter are adapted, with permission, from my piece 'Three Strands in Morality' in *W. J. M. M.: Political Questions. Essays in Honour of W. J. M. Mackenzie*, edited by Brian Chapman and Alan Potter (Manchester University Press, 1974).
2. The distinction of 'strands' is a different metaphor from my initial one of 'bands' in a spectrum. In that metaphor I tried to indicate how our moral thinking, the 'prism' through which we look, will cause us to see a diversity of factors to be taken into account. In the metaphor of 'strands' I try to indicate how certain different factors will enter into an actual viable form of social morality. Custom, Reciprocity and Generosity show ways in which distinctions in moral theory are illustrated in concrete morality. They do not however mirror the theoretic distinctions, since these are abstract ways of streamlining distinctions between factors which combine and influence each in various ways in practice. Custom combines uncritical use of principle with emotional approvals and disapprovals; Reciprocity is a critical use of principle guided by fairness: Generosity combines feeling with imaginative concern, and so fastens on the need for individual judgement. The teleological aspect of morality is implicit throughout, in that social morality is a way of defending and on occasion reforming a viable form of common life.
3. British moralists, particularly those of the eighteenth century, have traditionally used the term 'benevolence'. But since the eighteenth century, 'benevolence' has come to sound slightly avuncular. So I prefer to speak

of 'Generosity'. Hume indeed uses it as well as 'benevolence': rules of justice have become necessary because man has a 'confined generosity' (*Treatise of Human Nature* III, ii, 2). I am saying that even an unconfined generosity would not on its own provide a viable social morality.

4. See *The Open Society and its Enemies* (London, 1945) *passim*.
5. I suspect anarchists assume, without owning it, that someone is going to keep some sort of order going. If what they want is confined to spontaneous order in a small group, even this is probably not all that spontaneous. Decisions have to be talked over, and there will need to be some presumption that they will be carried out.
6. This has been brought out by Chester Barnard in *The Functions of the Executive* (Harvard, 1948).

CHAPTER 12

1. It is a direct challenge to the title 'The Only Possible Morality', a recent Paper by Ross Harrison in the *Aristotelian Society* Supp. Vol. L (1967). Ross Harrison tries to establish his case by a transcendental argument. I agree with the criticism of the second symposiast, Neil Cooper, on this.
2. Rudyard Kipling. 'In the Neolithic Age' in *The Seven Seas*.
3. W. G. Sumner, *Folkways* § 142ff. (Boston, Mass, 1907); R. Redfield, *The Little Community* (Chicago and Uppsala, 1955), p. 48.
4. *Freedom and Reason* (Oxford, 1963) pp. 113ff. For 'fanatics' see ibid., p. 105.
5. In *Contemporary British Philosophy* IV, edited by H. D. Lewis (London, 1974).
6. *Adam Smith's Science of Morals* (University of Glasgow, 1971). D. D. Raphael in the Dawes Hicks Lecture to the British Academy in 1972, 'The Impartial Spectator', (*Proceedings*, vol. LVIII), shows how Adam Smith repeatedly in later editions of the *Theory of the Moral Sentiments* tried to correct the impression that the approvals and disapprovals of the Impartial Spectator were simply the internalised ones of a social group, though these may well have been their sources. The 'love of praiseworthiness' is distinguished from the love of actual praise.
7. Cf. 'Ethical Absolutism and the Ideal Observer', *Philosophy and Phenomenological Research*, vol. XII, (1951—52), and vol. XV (1954—55). For Professor Brandt's view, see his *Hopi Ethics* (Chicago, 1954) and *Ethical Theory* (New York, 1959) and *Philosophy and Phenomenological Research*, vol. XV.
8. R. Brandt, *Hopi Ethics*, pp. 239—40.
9. I have argued this at some length in a paper 'Universalisability and Moral Judgment', *Philosophical Quarterly* vol. XIII (1953) and in my *Rules, Roles and Relations*, Ch. IV.
10. See p. 9.
11. Grice recognises that the whole of morality cannot be covered by this model by speaking of 'supererogatory' as well as basic obligations. His basic obligations are roughly those which I designated in my last chapter under 'Reciprocity' and those of supererogation under 'Generosity'.
12. See *A Theory of Justice* (Harvard and O.U.P., 1971). Rawls' view has been widely discussed, and also criticised. The most searching criticism in my opinion, is that by Brian Barry, in *The Liberal Theory of Justice* (Oxford, 1973). My own criticisms were given in a paper 'Justice' in the *Aristotelian Society* Supp. Vol. XLIII (1969), written on the basis of Rawls' earlier papers and before the book came out, but I stand by them.
13. C.U.P., 1967. Reprinted with two other kindred lectures on the same theme in *The Sovereignty of Good* (Routledge, 1970).

14. This is taken further in her Romanes lecture, *The Fire and the Sun* (Oxford, 1977) where the orientation towards Beauty seems to be more than a proxy, a leading into the orientation towards Good. This is indeed Platonic; it is a mystical orientation in which these words lose any separate meaning and become pointers to a perfection which cannot be specified in the images through which one tries to approach it.
15. Aristotle, *Nicomachean Ethics*, I, vi.
16. C. L. Stevenson, *Ethics and Language* (New Haven, 1944).
17. I have taken Utilitarianism to illustrate this maximising view. But it need not be assumed that the specifications or preferences to be maximised are thought of in terms of pleasure. The case stands for a view in which the dominant question is how to get the most of what we want, rather than to see what we can come to appreciate.
18. I take 'disinterestedness' to be a term for a disposition which is shown in e.g. (*a*) the effort after objectivity in appreciating a situation; (*b*) the pursuit of purposes which are not self-regarding; (*c*) the ability to take account of other people's interests as well as one's own.
19. Cf. *Summa Theologica* I i. quaestio 79, art. 13.
20. *The Foundations of Ethics* (Oxford, 1939) pp. 188ff.
21. In Chapter 9 I referred to Bernard Williams' treatment of such conflicts in his paper 'Moral Luck' (*Aristotelian Society*, Supp. Vol. L, 1976), where he says that 'Gauguin' could be justified by success in putting his art before the claims of his family; I differ from him in seeing this as a problem within morality and not between morality and something else, since I see morality as concerned with such judgements about priorities.

CHAPTER 13

1. Aristotle, *Rhetoric* I, xv, 1375.
2. For a fuller discussion of the difference between Natural Law and Natural Justice see my Essex Hall Lecture, *Justice and the Law* (Lindsey Press, 1963), where I supported the notion of Natural Justice, as a procedural virtue making fair judgements more likely, in preference to the notion of Natural Law with its connotation of a code.
3. *Iliad* 19: 86 and 137; cf. E. R. Dodds, *The Greeks and the Irrational*, p. 3.
4. *Hippolytus* 359—60; cf. Dodds, op. cit., p. 199.
5. Cf. St Thomas Aquinas, *Summa Theologica* II ii, quaestio 162 art. 3.
6. R. E. C. Browne *sub* 'Lust' in *The Dictionary of Christian Ethics* (London, 1967). The notes in the Dictionary on all the Seven Deadly Sins except Pride are by him. They are miniatures of ascetic theology.
7. I am indebted for this expression, 'the terrible strength of the saints', to the paper by Margaret Masterman, 'The Psychology of Levels of Will', in the *Proceedings of the Aristotelian Society*, 1947–8. I am also conscious in this chapter and elsewhere of many debts to conversations with her, especially as concerns the mystical basis of human development.
8. With the qualifications which I have already made, this could be taken as endorsing Bergson's view that there are 'two sources' of morality, the social which gives practical patterns of common life, and the 'mystical', which is an inner thrust in individuals, through which they can bring creative imagination and outgoing love into their relations with one another.
9. This *caveat* against the use of the term 'transformation', as standing for

something desirable without further qualification, does not apply to its use by Joan Miller in an article 'Transforming Activity' in *Theoria to Theory*, VIII, ii, which she is developing in a forthcoming book. She describes its cost.

10. *The Varieties of Religious Experience* (New York and London, 1902) p. 515.

Index